Herb Block

HERBLOCK SPECIAL REPORT

BY THE AUTHOR

Herblock Special Report

Herblock's State of the Union

The Herblock Gallery

Straight Herblock

Herblock's Special for Today

Herblock's Here and Now

The Herblock Book

HERBLOCK
SPECIAL
REPORT

Herbert Block

W · W · Norton & Company · Inc ·
New York

ISBN 0 393 08708 5

Copyright © 1974 by Herbert Block
FIRST EDITION

All Rights Reserved

Published simultaneously in Canada
by George J. McLeod Limited, Toronto

PRINTED IN THE UNITED STATES OF AMERICA

2 3 4 5 6 7 8 9 0

TO DOREE

ACKNOWLEDGMENTS

A few paragraphs are not enough to express adequately my appreciation to some of those who helped with this book: to Elisabeth Donovan, who researches with an almost clairvoyant sense of where to find things; to Lawrence Meyer and Barry Sussman for reading the text, particularly with eyes on the Watergate sections; to Haynes Johnson who interrupted his vacation to read the text and give helpful suggestions; and to Mary Lou Beatty who took time out of a tight schedule to do the same.

Bob and Jane Asher have gone through the texts of other books with me, and had the fortitude to take on this one too, and I can only say thanks again.

My appreciation goes also to James Mairs, of W. W. Norton and Company, for his remarkable production work.

I'm particularly indebted to Doree Lovell for going over the manuscript in several versions, each of which benefited from her expert editing.

I want to give special thanks to Jill Hammer for her valued work on all phases of the book; and to editor John Reistrup, who wields a pencil like a marshal's baton, bringing sentences into line and maneuvering paragraphs into order.

Finally, I want to express my gratitude and deep appreciation to Jean Rickard for her constant help and advice on every bit of manuscript, on research and editing, on page make-up—in short, on everything connected with this volume from beginning to end. Without her, this not only would be much less a book; it wouldn't have been done at all.

Herbert Block

CONTENTS

FOREWORD

Some time during Richard Nixon's tenure as Vice President one of his supporters wrote about what he called "the Dr. Fell syndrome" afflicting those who did not share his enthusiasm for Nixon. That was based on this variation of a seventeenth-century verse:

> I do not like thee, Dr. Fell.
> The reason why I can not tell;
> But this I know, and know full well,
> I do not like thee, Dr. Fell.

The idea was that those of us who questioned Nixon's fitness for public office had some mysterious quirk. The problem was not with him—it was with us.

That "Dr. Fell" theory was accepted by many who should have known better. There was more than enough "reason why" critics deplored Nixon's career. And it wasn't a matter of simply "not liking" him. It was not liking what he did, beginning with his first ugly campaign for Congress in 1946. If people who opposed what he did and what he stood for "could not tell," it was because there was so much to tell that it was hard to know where to begin.

Nixon was always the beneficiary of what, for want of a better term, might be called the Multiple Bad Things Advantage. There was too much to focus on easily and quickly; and this sometimes gave the impression that his critics were inarticulate or "disliked" Nixon for reasons "they could not tell." It also gave his supporters the opportunity to advance the idea that Nixon's critics opposed him because *he* was "against communism"—or because *they* were "anti-Republican"—or because *they* just didn't care for his face.

I found out about that Multiple Bad Things Advantage

when I spoke to audiences. Because I had done cartoons on Nixon since his days as a freshman congressman pushing "anti-subversive" legislation, I was long identified as being "anti-Nixon." And whatever the subject of my talk, in the question-and-answer periods that followed, someone would occasionally rise to ask what was wrong with Nixon. When this happened, I would generally reply with something like, "How much time have you got?"

Perhaps I should have answered such questions with a few well-organized facts about the Nixon career, even at the risk of boring some of the audience.

But this might not have done much good either. In 1968, when I took part in a radio talk program and a listener asked about Nixon, I went into some detail. To this the listener replied, "Oh, but that was long ago"—meaning before the latest campaign for public office.

The Multiple Bad Things record also made it difficult to note many legislative and policy activities of the Nixon administration that might otherwise have been subjects for comment. In a single speech there were often many statements that cried out for separate cartoons. And the scandals pushed aside other events, foreign and domestic, that would otherwise have deserved the space.

Even the scandals tumbled out in such profusion that *they* couldn't be covered adequately.

During the televised House Judiciary Committee debates on impeachment, the "Dr. Fell" gimmick and the Multiple Bad Things Advantage reached their ultimate extension. Congressmen defending Nixon kept demanding "specificity" —specific examples to support the charges of wrongdoing. One pro-Nixon congressman, attempting to show how difficult it would be for Nixon to respond to the charges, piled high onto his desk volume after volume of material painstakingly put together by the committee. Actually, it constituted a mountain of evidence. But few of the men and women committee members for impeachment were prepared instantly to deliver a mass of details, even if they could be allotted the time. Temporarily, at least, the appearance was given that "they could not tell" specifically what was wrong.

At the next day's hearings they came prepared, and began reading, line by line, some of the damning conversations from Nixon tapes. Finally the Nixon defender protested at *too much* "specificity" and called for an end to it.

But even when critics weren't tongue-tied by the mass of facts, they might be up against a stone-deaf nothing-wrong attitude. Always there was the implication that somehow there was something uncharitable about mentioning Nixon's misdeeds. For his apologists, everything was either too late: "Oh, that was the 'old' Nixon"; or too early: "But he hasn't been tried and found guilty yet"; and finally: "But now he's out of the White House!"

Before he became President, there was so much talk about forgetting the past that one would have thought he was being pursued by people who wanted to send him to the gallows. Actually, some of us were simply pointing out that his record did not recommend him for the highest office in the land.

During the impeachment inquiry, when the proposed article relating to tax fraud was being debated, one staunch Nixon defender on the committee asked indignantly whether the other members wanted to strip Nixon of everything he had.

What was being asked was simply that Nixon be treated like any other taxpayer, that he not be allowed to profit from his misdeeds, and that he be held accountable for his tax returns like anyone else.

After Nixon left office, the idea was still promoted that those who believed in letting the law take its course were somehow moved by personal motives. But quite the contrary was true.

It was not Nixon who had been assaulted by government, but the government that had been assaulted by Nixon.

It was not those who believed in the American system of justice who operated on a highly personal basis, but staunch Nixon supporters like Gerald Ford.

When President Ford recommended that Congress give former President Nixon large amounts of money—beyond all that was provided by law—and when he suddenly granted Nixon total and absolute pardon without even waiting for an indictment or a plea of *nolo contendere,* it was Ford who placed personal feelings for Nixon above his obligations to the people he was sworn to serve.

As for "personal" feelings, I only met Nixon a couple of times, and unintentionally. Once was at a large party when he was a congressman. The other time was at another large party early in the Eisenhower administration, when a White House aide literally grabbed my arm and insisted that I say hello to the Vice President. The conversations were brief and not unpleasant. There was no mention of differences, and there was nothing in the meetings to create personal dislike on either side.

This book obviously does not set out a complete record of the Nixon scandals or of the Nixon career. It doesn't even include all the cartoons about Nixon or relating to him—which probably number more than those I did on almost any other public figure (good or bad), including such long-in-the-limelight persons as Franklin D. Roosevelt and Joseph Stalin.

It does include a large number of the Nixon cartoons, along with dates of some incidents, and comments and recollections about their subject—a political career which in some way has affected all of us.

There is often confusion between fairness and favorableness. In 1974, Nixon supporters called for fairness to the President—or, in Nixonese, "the presidency."

I've believed in fairness to every President — and to 210 million American non-Presidents.

That's what all the fighting was about. It was summed up in the legal titles of the cases brought by the Special Prosecutor before the Supreme Court and printed in the usual court case manner:

United States of America, petitioner,

v.

Richard M. Nixon, President of the
United States

That's still what the fighting is all about—whether anyone who has gained office, however high, is above the people and the laws of the United States.

■

MEMBER
OF CONGRESS

When I came to Washington in 1946, it was a time of great change. After FDR and World War II, there were many new faces on the scene. And when the Republicans won control of Congress in the election that year, there were still more. 1946 also brought in some new Democratic congressmen, like John F. Kennedy.

1946

By the next election year, things were popping on all fronts. In early 1948 concern about foreign policy, the cold war, and communism rose sharply with the Soviet coup in Czechoslovakia and the beginning of the Berlin blockade.

1948

In May, there was divided opinion also on the newly created state of Israel, which our government recognized instantly, and which immediately found itself in a war with its neighbors.

At home, politics was never hotter. A beleaguered President Truman faced a "Dixiecrat" revolt in which politicians opposed to his civil rights program (which included an antilynching bill) were trying to devise ways to keep from him

13

the electoral votes of eleven southern states.

On his other flank, Truman was opposed by former Vice President Henry Wallace, who found Truman too conservative—particularly too much a cold-warrior. Wallace was already an unofficial third party candidate. And Republicans were counting on increasing their gains of the last election. Nevertheless, in May 1948, Truman was saying that there would be a Democrat in the White House during the next four years, and that he would be the man.

Probably nowhere in Congress was there more hostility toward him than in the House Committee on Un-American Activities, then near the peak of its power. It was demanding from the President an FBI "loyalty" report on Dr. Edward U. Condon, Director of the U.S. Bureau of Standards; and Truman was not about to open such files to a committee sitting in judgment on who was "American."

A freshman congressman on that committee declared that if Truman could withhold such information "that would mean that the President could have arbitrarily issued an executive order in . . . the Teapot Dome case, or any other case."

The congressman was Richard M. Nixon. He was achieving some prominence as the co-author of a bill sponsored by the Committee on Un-American Activities.

That was the Mundt-Nixon bill "to protect the United States against un-American and subversive activities." On May 16, while he was floor-managing that bill in the House, he made his first appearance in one of my cartoons ("We Got To Burn The Evil Spirit Out Of Her") along with committee colleagues Karl Mundt and Chairman J. Parnell Thomas.

At the top of page three in the same day's *Washington Post,* a news story began:

> Representative Richard M. Nixon (Rep. Calif.) asked Attorney General Clark yesterday to investigate alleged forgeries of signatures on congressional mail opposing the Mundt anti-Communist bill.
> "I called the FBI and discussed the situation with them

14

**"WE GOT TO BURN THE EVIL
SPIRITS OUT OF HER"**
May 16, 1948

at some length," he told reporters. "As a result I am asking the Attorney General for an opinion as to what action
can be taken. . . ."

In this news story, the forgeries are "alleged"; the young
congressman has associated himself actively with the FBI
and the Attorney General; and the story goes on to give nothing more than what Nixon said. He was doing very well with
the press.

That "anti-Communist" bill did not become law, however,
partly because of a stand taken by Republican presidential
candidate Thomas E. Dewey. Dewey was on record against
what he called "demagogic appeals to outlaw Communism
and destroy the Bill of Rights." He said, "In America we
prosecute people for what they do, not for what they think."

On May 17, Dewey debated a rival Republican presi-
dential contender, Harold E. Stassen. Stassen endorsed the
Mundt-Nixon bill and claimed that it would outlaw the
Communist Party. Dewey did not agree that it would have

15

this effect. He did not directly oppose the bill, which was about to pass the House of Representatives by an overwhelming vote. But he questioned its constitutionality, and pointed out that we already had twenty-seven laws "to deal with every conceivable act of subversion."

Dewey hit out at proposals to penalize people for their opinions or to outlaw any political party. He spoke of "this easy panacea of getting rid of ideas we do not like by passing a law" and said, "Stripped to its naked essentials, this is nothing but the methods of Hitler and Stalin. It is thought control borrowed from the Japanese war leadership. It is an attempt to beat down ideas with a club. It is surrender of everything we believe in."

Dewey's championing of civil liberties had an impact. The 1948 Mundt-Nixon bill died in the U.S. Senate. Much of Mundt-Nixon went into the 1950 McCarran Internal Security Act—which was eventually found to be almost wholly unconstitutional.

Although Nixon didn't come into my work until a day be-

"IT'S OKAY—WE'RE HUNTING COMMUNISTS"

October 31, 1947

"EVERYBODY READY FOR HALLOWE'EN?"

October 8, 1947

fore the Dewey-Stassen debate, he was not exactly unknown, and I had given considerable attention to the Committee on Un-American Activities of which he was an ambitious new member.

In 1948 the chairman of that committee was Rep. J. Parnell Thomas (R-N.J.) who later went to the federal penitentary for accepting kickbacks.

This committee, which itself had become something of a public spectacle, had an affinity for headlines and klieg lights. It took its investigative show on the road to Hollywood and later brought big name film people to Washington.

Committee members and their "friendly witnesses" found it objectionable for films to reflect problems in America. They suspected subversion if the character of a banker, for example, appeared in an unfavorable light; and Nixon was bothered about a movie like *The Grapes Of Wrath* being shown in Yugoslavia.

Despite these dim views, the committee was not able to find an actual "pro-Communist" film. But Nixon had a way

HOLLYWOOD STUFF
January 26, 1947

"IF YOU ASK ME, IT'S UN-AMERICAN"
October 22, 1947

around this. He asked film industry chiefs how many *anti-*Communist films they had produced in the past few years.

Here was a member of the U.S. Congress apparently judging American films by the standards of totalitarian countries —in which the arts are expected to serve the state and are measured in terms of how well they follow the line. In this case the "line" was that of a congressional committee.

After the film hearings, that committee turned its attention to many scientists who had contributed to our national defense. It made them targets of cold war fears by raising questions about their loyalty and security.

The most notable case was that of the Bureau of Standards director, Dr. Condon, an outstanding physicist whose work included important contributions to the development of radar and of the atom bomb.

In March 1948, the committee recklessly charged that Dr. Condon appeared to be "one of the weakest links in our

**"YOU'RE CONNECTED WITH
INFRA-RED RAYS, AIN'T YOU?"**
July 28, 1947

"I GOT A SECRET WEAPON TOO"
March 9, 1948

atomic security"—and then, for more than a year, denied him an opportunity to testify before it.

Dr. Condon was guilty of acting like a free American citizen at a time when the committee members seemed to think scientists should lock themselves up for fear of associating with the wrong people and risk spilling secrets. The committee asked not what scientists could do for their country but what they could do for its enemies. Since Dr. Condon simply went about his work of serving the United States without a special show of deference to what the committee would like, he was a prime subject for its wrath.

Many fellow-scientists, including Albert Einstein and Edward Teller, paid tribute to Dr. Condon; and President Truman supported him.

The Atomic Energy Commission, after the most searching scrutiny, declared it in the national interest that Dr. Condon be given continued clearance for his government work.

A few years later, there was a sequel to the committee's running war against this scientist. Dr. Condon had left gov-

**"AFTER AWHILE WE MAY
LET YOU TESTIFY"**
April 18, 1948

"HOW DID ATOMIC ENERGY INFORMATION LEAK OUT TO THE DAMN SCIENTISTS IN THE FIRST PLACE?"

September 12, 1948

"ANYBODY GOT A GOOD IDEA FOR A SUMMER SHOW?"

June 27, 1948

"FELLOWS, WE'VE GOT TO MEET THE COMPETITION"

April 28, 1950

ernment service to work in private industry on government-related projects, and Nixon—by then Vice President—learned that Dr. Condon had been given security clearance yet again. So Nixon interrupted his 1954 Western political campaign tour to phone Washington to have Dr. Condon's clearance withdrawn.

This harassment almost cost the U.S. another important Condon contribution. At the time, he was just completing the development of the nose cone, essential for our missile and space programs.

During that 1954 campaign, Nixon was still playing on fears of Communist subversion. But this was not something he had learned to do while a member of "the committee." He had used the method to get elected to Congress in 1946, when he defeated his able and conscientious predecessor, Jerry Voorhis, in a vicious campaign designed to make it appear that Voorhis was the candidate of Communists.

Later, when Sen. Joseph R. McCarthy (R-Wis.) began his fear-and-smear work, I made up a word that I needed in a

**THE DEVIL WAS SICK, THE DEVIL
A MONK WOULD BE**

December 30, 1948

**"YOU THE MAN THAT ORDERED
A WATCHDOG?"**

September 18, 1950

cartoon: McCarthyism. If Nixon had achieved sufficient prominence to be in the cartoons in 1946, the word might have been Nixonism. He was actually employing McCarthy tactics before McCarthy.

1950 Nixon and his old 1946 adviser, Murray Chotiner, used the same technique in his 1950 campaign for the U.S. Senate against Helen Gahagan Douglas. The campaign literature against Nixon's opponent included a "pink sheet" and she was dubbed "The Pink Lady." The literature and speeches suggested that she followed the "Communist line."

Readers who do not recall that period may hear a familiar voice, and some familiar phrases, in a 1950 Nixon campaign speech:

> At the start of this campaign, I am confronted with an unusual situation. My opponent is a woman. There are some whose experience I respect who have strongly advised that because she is a woman I should raise no questions as to her qualifications for the position she seeks. They say that to criticize a woman might lose the election.
>
> I have weighed this problem carefully and have reached a decision.
>
> My opponent *is* a woman. But she is also asking the people of California to send her as their representative to the United States Senate, where she could make decisions affecting their very lives. I say that the people of California are entitled to know *my* position on these issues, and I say they are entitled to know *hers as well*.
>
> I want my position to be crystal clear. There will be no name-calling, no smears, no misrepresentations in this campaign. *We* do not need to indulge in such tactics. But I say here and now that to the extent that Mrs. Douglas does not reveal, or conceals, her record, I feel that I have an obligation to expose that record to the voters of California so they can decide whether they want her to speak for them in the United States Senate.
>
> This is *one* election where the candidate will not fail to meet the issues head on.
>
> I have reached this decision because the record of my opponent disqualifies her from representing the people in the United States Senate.
>
> What are the qualifications that a United States Senator should have during this critical period of our history?
>
> Above all, it is necessary that he have a real under-

standing of the International Communist conspiracy at home and abroad. . . .

In addition to frontal assaults, the literature used in that 1950 Nixon campaign included an approach that would be used again later, in 1962 and 1972: material designed to appear as if it came from members of the opposition political party. A 1950 Nixon campaign mailing to registered Democrats began: "As one Democrat to another . . ."

The open Nixon literature described the campaign as a contest to determine whether America "shall continue to tolerate COMMUNIST CONSPIRACIES . . . persist in condoning BUREAUCRATIC PROFLIGACY and appeasing TOTALITARIAN AGGRESSION. . . ." Nixon had the support of racist demagogue Gerald L.K. Smith and Sen. Joseph R. McCarthy, who had leaped to prominence earlier that year by making sensational charges of Communists in government —which later proved unfounded. Both men campaigned for Nixon.

After less than four years in the House of Representatives, he was elected to the United States Senate. ■

SENATOR

Nixon's time in the Senate was a brief interlude between campaigns for higher office.

1952   Following his appearance in the cartoons as a congressman, Nixon did not turn up in them again until 1952, when he gained new prominence.

Elected as an Earl Warren delegate to the Republican National Convention—and serving as a member of the California delegation pledged to support Gov. Warren—Nixon undercut Warren. He worked instead for the nomination of Gen. Eisenhower. He became Eisenhower's running mate.

Nixon publicly spoke of President Truman, Secretary Dean Acheson and Gov. Adlai Stevenson as "traitors to the high principles in which many of the nation's Democrats believed." The emphasis was on the word *traitor* and the message got across.

As vice presidential candidate, Nixon supported "my good friend" Sen. Joseph R. McCarthy, who used the word "traitor" in connection with another highly respected fig-

24

ure. McCarthy called Gen. George C. Marshall "a living lie and a front man for traitors."

Nixon assailed presidential candidate Adlai Stevenson for supposedly having an undisclosed plan to end the Korean war. Nixon said that if Stevenson had a secret plan to end the war, this was a cruel hoax on the men fighting and dying in Korea.

Later on, when it would serve the purposes of presidential candidate Nixon, he would find reasons for not disclosing *his* ideas on how to end the Vietnam war.

Later on, Nixon—as President—would take bows for going to China and Russia. And when it served his purpose, he would speak admiringly of the late President Truman.

But in 1952 he was taunting the Truman administration for not being tough enough in its cold-war policies. In derogatory references to the Secretary of State, he spoke of

"MIDDLE OF THE ROAD"
August 25, 1952

"Acheson's Cowardly College of Containment." He sometimes referred to the "Truman-Acheson-Hiss policy."

He attacked the Truman administration as corrupt, and he
talked about cleaning up what he called "the mess in Washington" and of getting "pinks and Communists" out of government.

Nixon's campaign to clean up "the mess" came to a tem-
porary halt with the bombshell disclosure that he was the
recipient of a secret fund, contributed by a group of California businessmen, which had already put more than
$18,000 into his pocket. (The first figure to come out, used
in the Sept. 20 cartoon, was an underestimate).

The sum seems small compared to those involved in later
Nixon activities; and the new house which the secret fund
helped him acquire was no San Clemente estate. But the
$18,000 fund was a beginning. In those days—of what might

DEATH OF A SALESMAN
September 20, 1952

be called pre-Watergate morality—it did not take large amounts of cash or extremely valuable gifts to suggest wrongdoing.

There was no end to charges of corruption in the Truman administration after the acceptance of such things as a deep freeze and a mink coat. After pious outrage over these things, the disclosure of Nixon's secret fund was an embarrassment to his party; and there was a widespread demand that he be removed from the ticket. Gen. Eisenhower declared that his running mate must be "clean as a hound's tooth."

The Death-Of-A-Salesman cartoon did not mark the political demise of a candidate, but it did mark what logically seemed to be the end of that candidate as a "new-broom" salesman.

The Nixon response to demands for his removal from the ticket came not in placing the facts before Gen. Eisenhower, but in taking to television to deliver what became famous as his Checkers speech.

In this speech, delivered with his wife Pat sometimes sharing the screen as a silent and steadily-smiling onlooker, Nixon told of his humble beginnings, his wife's "respectable Republican cloth coat," and told of a gift he would not re-

"GOT TO KEEP THOSE OLD TEETH CLEAN"

October 28, 1952

"HERE, TOM—THIS WORKED FOR A FELLOW BACK IN '52"

June 15, 1967

A "Checkers speech" is still synonymous with attempted explanations of financial affairs by politicians.

turn: the cocker spaniel sent to his little daughters by a man in Texas. "And our little girl—Tricia the 6-year-old—named it Checkers."

Nixon has always been, to put it as nicely as possible, eclectic—ready to pick up anything that has worked for anyone else in politics, including those he most bitterly denounced. During Franklin Roosevelt's fourth campaign for President, FDR told of the charge that a special plane or ship had been ordered to transport his Scotch terrier Fala. With mock-seriousness, FDR said that he and his family were used to attacks, but that this charge of wastefulness had made Fala's Scotch blood boil.

In Nixon's dog act, "the kids, like all kids love this dog, and I just want to say this right now, that regardless of what they say about it, we are going to keep it."

I listened to this speech again a few years ago when it had a run in some neighborhood movie houses. It brought forth guffaws from a generation that hadn't heard it before. I was struck—as many others must have been—by the fact that the basic Nixon techniques have never varied.

There was the ostensible forthrightness (which was not really forthright) in seeming to make everything public without actually explaining anything. There was the suggestion that only through such outside contributions could a man of modest means like himself keep politics from being only for the wealthy—which did not explain the non-wealthy congressmen who *did* live within their government salaries and expense allotments.

There was the air of generosity and understanding toward people who—to hear Nixon tell it—would distort the truth.

There was the independent audit by a fine firm, which he received "just an hour ago . . . and I have that audit in my hand."

> But then I realized that there are still some who may say, and rightly so—and let me say that I recognize that some will continue to smear, regardless of what the truth may be—but that there has been understandably, some

28

"SIC 'IM, CHECKERS"

October 13, 1952

honest misunderstanding on this matter, and there are some that will say, well, maybe you were able, Senator, to fake this thing. How can we believe what you say—after all, is there a possibility that maybe you got some sums in cash? Is there a possibility that you might have feathered your own nest? And so now what I am going to do—and, incidentally, this is unprecedented in the history of American politics—I am going at this time to give to this television and radio audience a complete financial history, everything I have earned, everything I have spent, everything I own, and I want you to know the facts.

I will have to start early. I was born in 1913. Our family was one of modest circumstances, ...

He was "proud of the fact that the taxpayers, by subterfuge or otherwise, have never paid one dime for expenses which I thought were political and should not be charged to the taxpayers"—which didn't explain taking that secret-fund money, but sounded good. And: ". . . it isn't easy to come before a nation-wide audience and bare your life as I have done."

Nixon, who began by saying it would be morally wrong if any of that $18,000 went for his personal use, also asserted that no contributor "ever received any consideration he would not receive as an ordinary constituent. I just don't believe in that. . . ."

The late William Costello, an able correspondent, wrote about Nixon's fund (and fund administrator Dana Smith) in a 1960 book, *The Facts About Nixon*:

> Not the least serious aspect of the Checkers broadcast was Nixon's statement that he had never so much as made a telephone call to a federal office on behalf of a fund contributor. The *Washington Star* on September 24, the day after the broadcast, reported that Nixon's office had interceded on behalf of Dana Smith himself in a Justice Department case in which a firm owned by Smith's family was asking a tax rebate of more than a half a million dollars. Moreover, the legal opinion from Gibson, Dunn & Crutcher from which he quoted in the Checkers speech acknowledged that, after interviewing "a number of contributors," it had learned that "in two instances the

contributor had contacted Nixon to request his assistance in connection with matters pending before a department or agency of the government." Whether these inquiries were in the slightest measure reprehensible was not subsequently determined.

An important feature of the Checkers speech, which came to be a Nixon hallmark, was the diverting attack.

He challenged Gov. Stevenson and his running mate, Sen. John Sparkman (D-Ala.), to "come before the American people, as I have, and make a complete financial statement as to their financial history." And he declared, "if they don't, it will be an admission that they have something to hide." There was, of course, nothing to the effect that Gen. Eisenhower should make *his* finances public; there was still no real explanation of the secret Nixon fund; and still no complete Nixon financial record. (Stevenson then released photostatic copies of his tax returns for the past ten years—an example that Nixon declined to follow).

In the Checkers speech, Truman and Stevenson were attacked for the Korean war—being waged to prevent Communist expansion in Asia—and at the same time blamed for 600,000,000 people "lost" to the Communists.

Every part of the speech is filled with remembrances of things past and future.

There was the letter Nixon said he received, from a young war bride—"a letter which, after all this is over, no one can take away from us." And with it a contribution.

> Folks, it is a check for ten dollars, and it is one that I will never cash. And just let me say this. We hear a lot about prosperity these days, but I say, why can't we have prosperity built on peace rather than prosperity built on war? Why can't we have prosperity and an honest Government in Washington, D.C., at the same time?

(By 1974, some who re-read that question asked why we couldn't have either one.)

Then there were the comments on "smears"—against him, of course—and even then, in 1952, the attacks on the press:

Now, let me say this: I know that this is not the last of
the smears. In spite of my explanation tonight, other
smears will be made. Others have been made in the past.
And the purpose of the smears, I know, is this, to silence
me, to make me let up.

Well, they just don't know who they are dealing with.
I'm going to tell you this: I remember, in the dark days
of the Hiss trial, some of the same columnists, some of
the same radio commentators who are attacking me now
and misrepresenting my position, were violently opposing
me at the time I was after Alger Hiss. But I continued to
fight, because I knew I was right, and I can say to this
great television and radio audience that I have no apolo-
gies to the American people for my part in putting Alger
Hiss where he is today. And as far as this is concerned,
I intend to continue to fight.

Why do I feel so deeply? Why do I feel that in spite of
the smears, the misunderstanding, the necessity for a man
to come up here and bare his soul, as I have—why is
it necessary for me to continue this fight? And I want to
tell you why.

Because, you see, I love my country. And I think my
country is in danger. . . .

In this early assault on unnamed columnists and radio
commentators, the purpose of their "smears" was to make
him "let up" in his "fight" against people like Alger Hiss.

In fact, however, he had benefited enormously from the
press. Correspondent Bert Andrews, of the *New York Herald
Tribune* had aided Nixon on "the Hiss case" and helped cata-
pult him into headlines. The Hiss-Chambers court case came
about after a *Washington Post* reporter—Edward T. Folliard
—had asked Chambers, on a *Meet The Press* program, if he
would repeat on the air his charges against Hiss. After he did
so, *The Washington Post* said editorially that Hiss was
obliged to "put up or shut up" concerning the charges.

In his California campaigns Nixon had received the major support of the local and state newspapers, as he would
later receive the overwhelming support of the press in every
election in which he ever ran.

In the 1952 Checkers speech were words that twenty-two
years later would give the effect of an echo chamber: "I know
that you wonder whether I am going to stay on the Repub-

lican ticket or resign. Let me say this: I don't believe that I
ought to quit, because I am not a quitter."

And then, finally:

> But the decision, my friends, is not mine. I would do
> nothing that would harm the possibilities of Dwight
> Eisenhower to become President of the United States.
> And for that reason I am submitting to the Republican
> National Committee tonight through this television
> broadcast the decision which it is theirs to make.
>
> Let them decide whether my position on the ticket will
> help or hurt. And I am going to ask you to help them de-
> cide. Wire and write the Republican National Committee
> whether you think I should stay on or whether I should
> get off. And whatever their decision is I will abide by it.

The speech ended with Nixon (who wanted only to "drive
the crooks and the Communists and those that defend them
out of Washington") standing, looking intently into the

September 23, 1952

"Time for a Change" was the Republican slogan
in the campaign of 1946—the year Nixon was
elected to Congress.

**"HERE THEY COME DOWN
THE STRETCH"**

October 31, 1952

camera, and driving his fist forward as he said, "remember, folks, Eisenhower is a great man. Believe me, he is a great man. . . ."

But while the speech was larded with high praise for Gen. Eisenhower, Nixon left the decision for the Republican National Committee to make—and on the basis of response to his television appearance.

Through this technique, later used in other ways during greater Nixon scandals, Nixon sought to determine his own jury. The Republican National Committee reportedly received a huge volume of mail and telegrams overwhelmingly supporting Nixon. It might be that those impressed with his TV performance were more likely to write and wire than those who hooted at it.

"NAUGHTY NAUGHTY"
October 29, 1952

It is commonly assumed that the Checkers speech was a popular success. And perhaps it was. There was no Gallup Poll on it, so we'll never know what such a poll would have shown. The Associated Press reported widely differing newspaper editorial comments on the speech. And *The Washington Post*—which editorially supported Eisenhower for President—noted, in an article on reactions to the speech, that the calls it received were mixed.

Immediately after the Checkers speech, Eisenhower said he would not make a decision on the basis of a half-hour explanation. But following the Republican National Committee reports of a tremendous response, Eisenhower met with Nixon publicly and declared without any private discussion at all, "You're my boy." Nixon wept before the cameras and stayed on the ticket. What seemed good enough to impress a TV audience and the political professionals was good enough for Ike; and what was good enough for Ike was good enough for the country. In a wave of enthusiasm for Eisenhower, who was one of the most popular men ever to run for public office, Nixon became Vice President of the United States—a little more than six years after his first political campaign. ■

VICE PRESIDENT

1953

In a kind of "fire and fall back" rhythm, Nixon maintained a low political profile after the 1952 campaign, just as he did after the 1946 and 1950 campaigns.

Partly because of the new president and partly because of the headline activities of Senator Joseph R. McCarthy, the only mention of Nixon in the 1953 cartoons was in the caption of this one on Eisenhower "team" members.

"NOW KNOWLAND, NOW MARTIN,
NOW BRIDGES AND NIXON"
December 15, 1953

1954

There are a couple of cartoons which I've often been told I drew but never did.

One was said to have shown Nixon's face, with the line, "Would you buy a used car from this man?" I think this probably originated as a poster or postcard featuring a photo of the man, which would be better for the purposes than a cartoon. After the used-car line became well-known, however, I did a couple based on that theme.

The other cartoon which I never drew was supposed to have shown President Eisenhower and Vice President Nixon in front of the Capitol—some time after Ike's heart attack, and probably at their second inauguration. The caption supposedly had Nixon saying, "Race you to the top of the stairs." I first heard this told as a grim joke, and I don't recall ever seeing such a cartoon by anyone. It was one I certainly would not have done.

There is a third cartoon, though, that many people think I drew, which I *did* draw. That was the "sewer cartoon"—which is all that most people remember of it.

The time was 1954, when Nixon was campaigning for Republicans in over thirty states, generally by suggesting strongly that Democrats were Communist dupes or sympathizers.

"The Acheson policy," he said, "was directly responsible for the loss of China."

In this same year he had said of Secretary Dulles—and in derogation of men like George C. Marshall and Dean Acheson —"Isn't it wonderful finally to have a Secretary of State who is not taken in by the Communists?"

Having started out using the methods of McCarthyism before McCarthy, Vice President Nixon was now practicing it on a grand scale at the very time McCarthy himself was on the skids.

In his campaign speeches, Nixon said that when the Eisenhower administration came in, "we found in the files" a "blueprint for socializing America." His aides explained from time to time that he was merely referring figuratively to policies Truman proposed.

He said: "We've been kicking out the Communists, the fellow travelers and the security risks by the thousands." One of the gimmicks here was the category "security risks." These could include people fired from their jobs on charges with no more foundation than an allegation from an unknown informant that they drank too much or held dangerous opinions.

As for "the Communists" and "fellow travelers," the chairman of the Civil Service Commission (an Eisenhower appointee) found no evidence of any Communists or fellow travelers having been discovered or dismissed.

But that was not all. It also turned out that about half of those "risks" who were fired, had been *hired* by the Eisenhower administration.

When Adlai Stevenson pointed out that the Soviet economy was growing at a faster rate than our own, Nixon re-

37

plied by accusing Stevenson of spreading pro-Communist propaganda. Nixon said: "His (Stevenson's) dislike for our economic system is his own business, but when he links such criticism with praise of the rapid growth of the Soviet economy, he is performing a grave disservice to us. . . ."

Incredibly, only three and a half years later, Nixon was himself pointing out that the Soviet economy was growing faster than ours.

A good example of his technique in campaigning against Democratic congressional candidates was in his treatment of moderate Sen. Joseph C. O'Mahoney (D-Wyo.). O'Mahoney had lost his seat in the Eisenhower landslide of 1952 and was now running for the Senate again. Meanwhile, in 1953, he had performed legal services for the United States-Cuban Sugar Council—a matter of public record. Nixon, in the context of his 1954 "anti-Communist" campaign, referred to O'Mahoney as a "foreign agent."

"All over the United States," said Nixon in his speeches, "the Communists are in the forefront calling for the defeat of Republican candidates."

While Nixon went from city to city and state to state smearing reputable and responsible legislators such as Sens. Richard Neuberger (D-Ore.) and O'Mahoney and Rep. John

"HERE HE COMES NOW"
October 29, 1954

"AH, YES—ISN'T THAT FELLOW McCARTHY TERRIBLE?"
July 2, 1954

Carroll (D-Colo.), it occurred to me that he was figuratively criss-crossing the country by sewer. Hence the cartoon, "Here He Comes Now."

A question that sometimes comes up is whether there are any cartoons I regret drawing—and this is sometimes asked after some mention of the sewer cartoon. The answer is none that stands out in my mind, although if I were to go over a few decades of work, there undoubtedly would be some I might have done differently. However, the manhole cartoon would not be one of those.

The only problem with this cartoon was that some people and publications—often Nixon supporters—later wanted to reprint it out of context. I learned to require that they run a type-line beneath it giving the year and the circumstances when it was drawn.

From the summer of 1973 onward, there were no more problems about the 1954 "sewer cartoon" being taken out of context. I received many requests from people who wanted to see it reprinted either with or without the date and type-line, because they felt it was pertinent.

It was around 1954 that Nixon publicly complained about my cartoons. He had previously cancelled his subscription to *The Washington Post* because of them. There is even a story that his cancellation came some time before *The Post* acquired its morning rival, the *Washington Times-Herald*, and took over that newspaper's subscription list—and that he then had to cancel again to avoid getting *The Washington Post* and *Times-Herald*, with the same cartoons. It's a good story, but I've never been able to verify the part about the second cancellation.

In his famous press conference after his defeat in 1962, Nixon made an oblique reference to President Kennedy's cancellation of the *New York Herald Tribune*. He said, ". . . unlike some people, I've never cancelled a subscription to a newspaper." This was not so.

Chalmers M. Roberts, long a correspondent for *The Washington Post*, provided a postscript on this subject. In his book, *First Rough Draft*, Roberts wrote of a December

1959 interview with Nixon, which began at the Nixon home and continued on the ride to the office in the vice presidential Cadillac.

> There was an odd addition to the conversation as we rode along that day. Nixon asked me to tell the *Washington Post*'s cartoonist, Herblock, that he really thought he was great. But he said he did not get the *Post* delivered at home because of Herblock's cartoons . . . "I don't want the girls to be upset". . . But, he added, he read the *Post* as soon as he got to his office. Then, reflecting on Herblock's drawings of him, he commented: "You know, a lot of people think I'm a prick, but I'm really not."

The comments were, as Roberts noted, rather odd. Perhaps he had some admiration for persistence in others. Maybe he just figured there was nothing to lose and everything to gain by passing along a compliment on my work.

At times Nixon referred more angrily to what it was like to have his children see my cartoons. I wonder if he ever thought what it must have been like for Helen Gahagan Douglas and other political figures whose patriotism and

"CARRY ON, LADS"
October 7, 1954

DICKEY
October 26, 1954

character he cleverly put under suspicion—and how it was for *their* children.

In her book, *Private Faces/Public Places,* Abigail Mc-Carthy referred to attacks on the "patriotism and loyalty" of her husband—then Rep. Eugene McCarthy (D-Minn.)—by Warren Burger (now Chief Justice). She also told of full-page newspaper ads—signed by prestigious St. Paul lawyers—headed, IS YOUR CONGRESSMAN A TRAITOR? She wrote:

> Ellen, who started kindergarten that fall, came home
> the first week and said to me piteously, "Mama, what is
> a Communist?" And I knew that some child on the play-
> ground had told her that her father was one.

This kind of campaigning by Nixon and those who followed his lead, prompted cartoons like that of the manhole.

As for his reactions to them, the stories varied. I recall a couple of articles which appeared almost simultaneously in different magazines by members of his family—maybe ghost-written or perhaps "as told to." I think one was supposedly by his mother and the other by his wife. Anyhow, in one of the articles he would not allow my cartoons in his house; and in the other article, "Dick" had such a great sense of humor that he clipped my cartoons and put them up on the walls at home.

In a satirical vignette of the Nixons sitting by the fireside at home, Mort Sahl once got off one of his most telling lines. He described Pat knitting an American flag, while Dick reads the Constitution—looking for loopholes.

1955

When the cartoon dated Sept. 25, 1955 appeared, that day's paper also carried the news of President Eisenhower's heart attack. Of course, the cartoon was drawn and being printed before the news came in. But without the aid of a crystal ball, the only way to prevent such a coincidence would be to avoid criticizing all prominent figures on the chance that any of them might be stricken at any time. Nevertheless, there were some who deplored the "timing" of this cartoon.

As a result of the Eisenhower illness, Nixon gained added prestige. There was now not only the possibility that the Vice President might later be nominated for President, but that he might succeed to the top spot before the Eisenhower term was finished. From then on, he faced less opposition within his own party.

1956

Before the 1956 Republican convention, there was a move to "dump Nixon" and replace him with a vice presidential candidate less offensive to many in both parties. But the President, who had thought Nixon might be satisfied with a Cabinet post in a second Eisenhower administration, let Nixon "chart his own course." Unsurprisingly, Nixon opted for the vice presidential candidacy again—and campaigned extensively for re-election.

**"SWEETEST LITTLE FELLER
—EVERYBODY KNOWS—"**

January 14, 1955

**"YOU'RE GOING TO RUN AGAIN
AREN'T WE?"**

September 25, 1955

As part of Nixon's continuing attack on Adlai Stevenson, who was again the Democratic presidential candidate, Nixon termed Stevenson's proposals for nuclear arms control to be "catastrophic nonsense."

Nixon had earlier suggested the introduction of American troops into Indochina; and he managed to be more fiercely

"LET'S SEE—WHAT'LL I WEAR TODAY?"

February 15, 1956

anti-Communist-China than Secretary of State John Foster Dulles.

A political observer can only wonder what charges of "catastrophic" blundering Nixon would have charged to any member of the opposition party who had made possible a Russian wheat deal and Russian nuclear parity, or who had appeared to be chummy with the leaders of "Red China."

"NOW YOU KIDS BEAT IT"
October 26, 1956

"YOU SAID IT, PAL—WE BOTH GOT A RIGHT TO POISON THE AIR"

October 5, 1956

1957 -58

When Russia launched its first "sputniks" in 1957, Americans who had felt that we must naturally be first in everything were somewhat shaken. This happened during the Eisenhower-Nixon administration, and there were no spy scares or accusations of treason. What we had instead were some examples of the Offensive Defense, which I described in a book at that time:

> The most interesting statements of all came from the Vice-President, who said that the government would have to finance a satellite-and-missile program by making sharp cuts in domestic spending. He made a stirring speech telling Americans to get away from their weeping walls and to get behind our missile people and help them. 'We've got work to do,' he said. 'Let's get on with it like Americans.' That certainly sounded affirmative, except that you got the feeling he was talking to the wrong fellows. Unless he had expected us average guys to build satellites in our back yards, there wasn't much we could do to get on with the job. It was really the men running the government who should have been doing that.

"CAREFUL, MEN—DON'T BREAK THE FURNITURE"
September 20, 1957

SUNSHINE
November 6, 1957

Oh, but he was a good talker, though. No, I wouldn't say he made you forget your troubles, exactly. He just sort of made you forget that he and his friends had anything to do with them.

That talk went so well that a little later he made one to the American Football Coaches Association, possibly figuring that they should *punt* something into space for us. . . .

'This is no time to get out the crying towel or to throw in the sponge,' he said. And it was grand to hear such vigorous statements. Of course, here again, it was a little as if somebody on a fumbling football team had walked over to the stands and reprimanded the audience for not cheering enough. But it sounded fine. And he warned against anybody making a political football out of security. That was particularly impressive because it wasn't coming from some theoretical dreamer or idle observer. We knew we were getting it straight from a fellow who had plenty of experience at making political footballs out of security. . . .

He wound up his speech with a defense of American scientists; and it was thrilling. It just made you itch to get at those darned American People who were attacking our scientists. But this feeling wore off after a while. When you stopped to think about it, the American people weren't attacking our scientists at all; they were complaining about an Administration that had not made proper use of our scientists. And when you stopped to think about it a little more, you remembered that top scientists like Condon and Oppenheimer had been driven out of government service by politicians like the Vice-President himself. But it would have been a pity to spoil such grand oratorical performances by analyzing what was said.

The Vice-President was a master at performing the difficult maneuver which might be called Fleeing The Scene Of The Crime Until They Catch Up With You, And Then Standing Up In The Stirrups And Crying, 'Forward, Men!' And that's one that takes real skill.

An endless succession of "new" Nixons kept turning out to be the same Nixon as before. And it occurred to me that we never had to have a "new" Lincoln or a "new" Roosevelt or a "new" anyone worthwhile in high public office.

But there was a desire to believe that with the progression to higher offices, a beneficial change was taking place. It was

"OF COURSE, IF I HAD THE TOP JOB I'D ACT DIFFERENTLY"

October 16, 1958

always argued that with increasing responsibilities (and higher positions) he would grow—and, of course, if he reached the highest position, he would grow to true greatness. The ideas of change and "growth" were peddled assiduously. Chameleons change color—but they remain chameleons. Sharks grow—and so do their appetites.

The cartoon of Oct. 16, 1958 ("Of Course, If I Had The Top Job . . .) summed up the view which I have always held, that Nixon was unqualified by character for high public office, and that in the 1950s he had already gone much higher than he should have.

Earlier that year, Margaret Halsey wrote a prophetic article, in which she said:*   . . .

> Mr. Nixon has no more altered in character or personality structure because he is close to the Presidency than Harry Truman has altered in character or personality structure by reason of having left it.
>
> To be sure, Mr. Truman was by his own admission unprepared, in terms of world statesmanship, to enter upon the Presidency, whereas Mr. Nixon has been conscientiously readying himself for the office. But Mr. Truman was not *morally* unprepared for the White House. Mr. Nixon, on the other hand, suffers from a disability that all the briefing in the world will not mitigate. He cannot go back to Sunday School.
>
> The point is a pivotal one. If the Vice President's energies are truly as monumental as the Luce publications and others in the swelling chorus say they are, then the Presidency in its present form may prove too narrow for them. Mr. Nixon, as President, may wish to extend the powers of his office the way those other dark-jowled fellows—the ones in South America—so often do. The opposition—the people who think that such an Executive should not overbalance the Legislature and the Judiciary—must then expect to get the "old" Nixon treatment. . . . more and more respectable and intelligent people will gradually be drawn over to the side of condoning, forgiving and forgetting. It will get lonelier and lonelier to criticize and speak the truth.
>
> And indeed one can understand why. Should Mr.

* "Beware the Tender Trap," *New Republic*, Jan. 13, 1958.

Nixon succeed to the Presidency, it will be a great temptation to make exonerating noises about him. To live with him as President, in full awareness of what his actions have shown him to be, will require considerable endurance. One's natural instinct will be to set up a sheltering illusion—to warm up the bleak and wintry truth by arguing that he cannot *really* be so bad. There will be a disposition to believe that merely sitting in an office with the American flag and the Great Seal of the United States has an ennobling effect. Or being the father of two. And so they do—but not on confirmed and habitual self-promoters.

Forced to adjust to Mr. Nixon as Chief Executive, many people will automatically develop a sort of selective morality. They will have one set of ethics—the one they were taught as children and have been used to all their lives—for judging themselves and their friends. They will have another, and a much lower one, for the President of the United States.

At first glance, this might seem like a workable compromise; but it is not. Gresham's Law operates just as immutably in ethics as it does in economics, and cheap morals tend to drive good morals out of circulation. To charitable souls, it may seem vindictive to dwell on Mr. Nixon's past, but the issue transcends considerations of charity. To remember the Vice President's record is to keep alive—if only by inversion—that standard of morality which makes life worth living.

. . .

Even in 1958, Nixon found nothing wrong in the Sherman Adams-Bernard Goldfine scandal which finally caused Eisenhower to drop Adams, who was his chief aide. Later, when Nixon was President, he would say to his aides: "That's what Eisenhower—that's all he cared about. He only cared about—Christ, 'Be sure he was clean.' Both in the fund thing and in the Adams thing. But I don't look at it that way."

In teaching others members of his party how to campaign, Nixon always stressed that "the public memory is short"—a tenet that he relied on throughout his long career.

**"IF YOU GET IT, REMEMBER
I MENTIONED IT"**

March 23, 1958

**"GEE, FELLOWS, THIS IS FUN, BY
THE WAY, WHO ARE THE REST OF
THE BOYS?"**

October 23, 1958

"YOU OBVIOUSLY RECOGNIZE OUR SUPERIOR FACILITIES FOR PUTTING THINGS INTO ORBIT"

July 28, 1959

"WELL, THERE WE WERE IN THIS MODEL KITCHEN, AND—"

August 5, 1959

1959

The Nixon trip to Russia and the "kitchen debate" with Khrushchev took place in 1959. As photographers snapped pictures, Nixon pointed what seemed to be a stern finger at Khrushchev. On his return from the trip, Nixon gave the American television audience an account of it —in which, as he presented it, he came out quite well.

When Secretary of the Interior Stewart Udall visited Russia during the Kennedy Administration, Khrushchev told him that he could have his picture taken shaking a finger in the same manner.

"YOU SUPPOSE KHRUSHCHEV KNOWS MORE ABOUT THE 1960 RACE THAN WE DO?"

December 7, 1958

August 9, 1959

**"WE'VE GOT TO TAKE
THE LONG VIEW"**

January 5, 1960

**"COME ON, COME ON—
HURRY IT UP"**

May 24, 1960

**"SUMMITRY IS A SILLY BUSINESS
ANYHOW—LATELY"**

June 2, 1960

Shortly before these cartoons appeared, the planned Eisenhower-Khrushchev meeting blew up due to the U-2 spy plane incident.

1960 In *The Making of the President* (*1960*), Theodore White wrote that when some Republicans criticized Nixon for his "kid-glove" campaign against Kennedy, he was reported to have said, "I have to erase the Herblock image first."

In this presidential campaign I made a little change in the drawing of the Nixon face to note that he found it advisable to operate personally at a somewhat higher level than before.

I covered the dark jowls with a mask that tied behind his head with strings. Later on, I eliminated the strings and drew a kind of sharp stylized hairline meant to suggest the mask. In some cartoons there were several masks—sometimes with several Nixons behind them.

The Nixon theory that "the public memory is short" may have been correct. But in 1960, the public memory still re-

**"MIRROR, MIRROR, ON THE WALL,
WHO'S THE FAIREST
ONE OF ALL?"**

January 2, 1960

tained images of the earlier Nixons—a disadvantage which would diminish by 1968, when he would have the benefit of several years of public forgetfulness.

The biggest feature of the 1960 campaign was the televised Kennedy-Nixon "debates"—which were actually answers to panel members' questions given on shared platforms. Nixon—who had two top television advisers and his own make-up man—wrote later that the difficulty with his campaign was that he focused too much on substance and not enough on appearance.

Fourteen years after the Kennedy-Nixon debates—at a time when the public was aware of taped Nixon conversations and of expletives deleted—a few newspapermen refreshed the public memory of some Nixon comments in those 1960 exchanges. Said the then-Vice President, in an

**"WILL THE REAL RICHARD NIXON
PLEASE STAND UP?"**

June 9, 1960

"WELL, YOU OUGHT TO KNOW ABOUT 'GROWTHMANSHIP'"

June 30, 1960

"WE HOPE YOU DIDN'T GET THE IMPRESSION THAT WE DON'T HAVE ANY USE FOR YOU"

July 21, 1960

NEW FRONTIER

August 7, 1960

GREAT DEBATE

October 2, 1960

obvious slap at former President Truman:

> One thing I have noted as I have traveled around the country are the tremendous number of children who come out to see the presidential candidates. I see mothers holding up their babies so they can see a man who might be President of the United States. I know Sen. Kennedy sees them, too. It makes you realize that whoever is President is going to be a man that all children of America look up to or look down on, and I can only say I am very proud that President Eisenhower restored dignity and decency and, frankly, good language to the conduct of the presidency of the United States.
>
> And I only hope should I win this election that I could approach President Eisenhower in maintaining the dignity of the office, and see to it that whenever any mother or father talks to his child, he can look at the man in the White House, and whatever he may think of his policies, he will say, "Well, there is a man who maintains the kind of standards personally that I would want my child to follow."

**"A LITTLE CLOSER—NOT TOO
CLOSE—SMILE—THAT'S IT"**

July 27, 1960

**"AND BESIDES, THOSE
GRAPES ARE SOUR"**

August 4, 1960

**"I HARDLY TOUCH THE STUFF
MYSELF, ANY MORE"**

August 23, 1960

COALITION

October 11, 1960

**"WHICH FACE AND WHAT
OPINIONS WILL DICK PUT ON
NEXT? TUNE IN AGAIN . . ."**

October 16, 1960

After the close 1960 election, a story began—and still goes on—that Nixon had been cheated out of the presidency by crooked vote-counting, but that he had conceded the election to John F. Kennedy to avoid keeping the country in suspense or dividing it, while votes in some areas were re-counted. But the evidence of this "generosity" always gets back to Nixon's own words.

There is nothing in Nixon's career, from his 1946 congressional election to his forced resignation from the presidency, to bear out the idea that he would concede anything he thought he might possibly win or keep.

My recollection—shared by several others with long memories—is that there was much talk of stolen votes in Cook County and possible demands for a re-count. But when it was suggested that there be a re-count of the votes for the entire state of Illinois—including the Republican-dominated down-

"SELDOM HAS A CANDIDATE HAD SO MUCH EXPERIENCE AT NOT BEING RESPONSIBLE FOR DECISIONS"

August 25, 1960

At the presidential press conference of August 24, when Eisenhower was asked, "What major decisions of your administration has the Vice President participated in?", Ike considered this question and replied, "If you give me a week, I might think of one."

state area—the Nixon camp lost its enthusiasm for going over the ballots again.

Such recollections might be disputed. What is harder to dispute is the 1960 electoral vote: Kennedy, 303; Nixon, 219. Taking away Illinois' twenty-six electoral votes and giving them to Nixon would have left the loser still losing by thirty-two electoral votes.

While benefiting from the story of a magnanimous refusal to demand vote re-counts, Nixon nevertheless kept alive the idea that he was cheated. This was hardly the action of a man who wanted to avoid bitterness and who put the national interest above self.

Nixon, mind you, was not suggesting that crooks had stolen his election. He was simply quoting little Julie as asking daddy when were they going to have a re-count in Cook County.

Whether it's in accepting results, taking personal responsibility, or showing some originality or spontaneity, there are little incidents which afford interesting contrasts between Presidents.

After John F. Kennedy was elected President, he was asked what his favorite song was, and replied that he liked

"AND NOW A WORD TO YOU-ALL
FROM OUR LITTLE
OLD LOCAL SPONSOR—"
November 4, 1960

"FOLKS—WAIT—LISTEN—"
November 2, 1960

"Hail to the Chief" pretty well. Eight years later when President Nixon was making the rounds of his inaugural parties he would tell the celebrants there that since he had become President, people often asked him what his favorite song was; and (with a little laugh), he said he told them that he liked "Hail to the Chief" pretty well.

A section covering the Kennedy-Nixon election can not be complete without a Nixon quote from *Six Crises* on their post-election meeting. (It's interesting that many people think the title of that book is *MY Six Crises*—which is what they were).

> I then brought up an issue which I told him was one on which I had particularly strong views—the recognition of Red China and its admission to the UN. I did so because just the day before, Senator George Smathers had told me that Chester Bowles and some of Kennedy's other foreign policy advisers were urging him to reappraise our position on that issue. . . .
>
> In expressing my strong opposition to this policy, I pointed out that the issue wasn't whether Red China had one vote in the Assembly, or even the veto power. What was really at stake was that admitting Red China to the United Nations would be a mockery of the provision of the Charter which limits its membership to "peace-loving nations." And what was most disturbing was that it would give respectability to the Communist regime which would immensely increase its power and prestige in Asia, and probably irreparably weaken the non-Communist governments in that area.

In 1971, President Nixon went on television to announce his forthcoming visit to China—which shortly afterward would have a seat on the U.N. Security Council.

"Non-Communist governments in that area," like our ally Japan, were shocked that they had not even been given advance notice of the announcement. ■

OUT OF OFFICE

1962

The Nixon campaign for governor of California in 1962 publicly brought Nixon together again with Murray Chotiner, who had worked on Nixon's campaign strategy from his first congressional campaign in 1946. The tactics these two made famous were once more brought into play and produced a second "sewer cartoon."

An AP news story of the period gives something of the flavor of that campaign:

> SAN FRANCISCO, Oct. 4 (AP)—Two Democratic State Assemblymen have denied Richard M. Nixon's charge that they helped lead the riot against the House Un-American Activities Committee in San Francisco in May, 1960.
>
> Assemblymen John O'Connell and Phillip Burton, both of San Francisco, said they were nowhere near the city hall when the riots occurred. Both oppose the committee and had spoken to a students' rally at Union Square the day before.
>
> Mr. Nixon, Republican nominee for Governor, made the charge Monday during a joint appearance with Gov. Edmund G. Brown before an editors' meeting in San Francisco. Departing from the rules, he asked Gov. Brown directly if he were supporting the two. . . .

September 25, 1962

**"OOPS—WRONG BAG
OF TRICKS"**

March 29, 1962

When President Kennedy spoke at the University of California in 1962, and came accompanied by his brother Robert, Nixon called them "carpetbaggers." Many recalled President Eisenhower's travels in 1960 and the barnstorming tours of Vice President Nixon in off-year campaigns. Most people did not think of the President of the United States as a carpetbagger in any state.

Three days before that news story, Mr. Nixon was assuring voters of California that "I have made mistakes but I am an honest man."

He also told the voters that the strategy of the opposition was "to have a new false charge issued every day so that the truth could never catch up with the falsehood," that Gov. Brown would launch "the most massive campaign of fear and smear in the history of California politics"—and declared later that "this campaign of smear against me and abuse against my family has reached a point where I can no longer ignore it."

In that 1962 campaign there were partial previews of

1972. There were cropped pictures of Gov. Brown altered to substitute people not originally photographed with him— and accompanied by "statements" he had not made.

There was a postcard mailing to Democratic voters purporting to be written by Democrats concerned for the future of their party. According to the mailing (which began, "This is not a plea for any candidate . . ."), they were trying to save the party from left-wing control and were soliciting contributions from fellow Democrats.

This material—from the "Committee for the Preservation of the Democratic Party in California"—was actually prepared and mailed as part of the Nixon campaign.

Nixon's campaign manager was H. R. (Bob) Haldeman, who later became his White House chief of staff. Also associated with management of this campaign was Herbert Kalmbach, the Nixon lawyer, who, in 1974, was convicted for illegal fund raising.

The 1962 mailing became the subject of a lawsuit filed by California State Democratic leaders, who won a judgment handed down in 1964 by Judge Byron Arnold, of the San Francisco County Superior Court of California.

In his ruling the judge said: "The paramount purpose for organizing the Committee for the Preservation of the Democratic Party in California and its related postcard poll and activities was to obtain from registered Democrats votes and money for the campaign of Richard M. Nixon."

Judge Arnold's ruling also said that "Mr. Nixon and Mr. Haldeman approved the plan and project . . . and agreed that the Nixon campaign committee would finance the project." This campaign effort, which violated the California State Election code, cost something over $70,000 paid to a polling and fund-raising outfit. But in its "campaign statement" filed with the California Secretary of State, Nixon's campaign listed the money for the fraudulent mailing as "expenditures for payment of personnel."

The actual postcard mailed was, the judge found, "re-

·viewed, amended, and finally approved by Mr. Nixon personally."

Nixon later brought with him to the White House many members of the 1962 campaign group. They knew the kind of work he wanted done; and he knew they would *do* the kind of work he wanted done.

Nixon supporters later asserted that as President, he was guilty only of "mistakes of judgment" in selecting some of his associates. This was like saying that a mobster had made mere errors of judgment in hiring friends who happened to carry sawed-off shotguns in their violin cases. How could he guess they were not actually going around conducting musicales?

After his 1962 defeat, Nixon held what he called "my last press conference," in which he told newsmen, ". . . just think how much you're going to be missing. You won't have Nixon to kick around any more. . . ."

That brought a bad reaction even from *Time* magazine, which, under the direction of Henry Luce, had been all-out in its support of Nixon and violent in attacks on his critics. *Time* published an article titled "Career's End," in which it said that Nixon's admirers could only agree that "his character was flawed." This article added that the post-election press conference left little more to be said about Richard Nixon. A television network did an "obituary" on his career. I did nothing at all on his defeat, and hoped there was indeed nothing more to be said—or drawn—about him.

Less well-known than the "last press conference" was the grace note with which Nixon expressed appreciation to those who had worked for him in 1962:

> . . . our 100,000 volunteer workers I was proud of. I think they did a magnificent job. I only wish they could have gotten out a few more votes in the key precincts; but because they didn't, Mr. Brown has won and I have lost the election.

"HE SAYS THAT AFTER THE BLOODLETTING HE CAN BRING US PEACE"

November 17, 1963

In November, 1963, Nixon pictured himself not as a 1964 candidate, but as a healer after the "blood-letting" of the battle for the nomination was over. Nevertheless, at the 1964 Governors Conference he made an effort to promote himself for the nomination.

"PARDON ME, DID YOU KNOCK?"

March 17, 196.

"AS A LAWYER, I'D BE GLAD TO HELP YOU MAKE OUT A WILL"

April 16, 1964

"GEE, THAT WAS A TOUGH BREAK

May 19, 196

More than most politicians, Nixon was a professional political candidate, for whom running and winning were everything. Even after 1962, he was Mr. Available, still working toward whatever would best advance his prospects. Following Goldwater's 1964 primary victory in California, Nixon promoted an anti-Goldwater effort which failed—and then quickly shifted to a pro-Goldwater stance. After the convention, he went down the line for Goldwater. Four years later this would pay off.

During this period I drew Nixon as a vulture and, more often, as an undertaker. It seemed to fit his manner and his hopes for political gain, which rested largely on seeing others falter or fall.

In 1966, after Nixon began his comeback as a presidential candidate through a televised reply to remarks by President Johnson, I wrote a piece which I later included in a book. It appears again here because it represents, as well as I've been able to capture it in words, what seems to me to be the essential and constant Nixon.

CALIFORNIA
May 29, 1964

June 17, 1964

The Salesman

Good evening, madam. My name is Rick Mixon. No, please don't get up. Just let me walk over here, make a slight turn and sit down casually but sincerely on the edge of this desk, and look at you in a friendly but earnest way. And permit me to make one thing crystal clear at the very beginning. I am with you for the sole purpose of helping you. However deep your grief, and I know it is very deep indeed, I feel it is important that you recognize and never forget that one simple fact.

You have lost a loved one, and you are distraught, and you are being tugged this way and that, and you are asking, "What shall I do? To whom can I turn?" These are perfectly natural questions, and as I lean slightly forward and fold my hands sincerely let me say that I think I can answer them for you. You need, first of all, someone that you can trust. That is why I am here. And, secondly, you need the best casket you can afford.

I know that the grocer, the doctor and others are trying to divert you to other things, other ways of allocating your precious but limited resources. And let me say without malice but simply for the record that I am shocked at their incredible irresponsibility and callousness and pettiness in discussing your personal welfare at such a time. Let me speak plainly, and let the record be straight on this—the question you face today is a clear and simple one: How much do you want to do in memory of one who meant much to you?

The decision, briefly, is whether you want the twenty-thousand-dollar casket or whether you feel that the seventeen-thousand-dollar casket (without a top) or the twelve-thousand-dollar casket (of damp cardboard) is good enough. The decision is yours and yours alone. All that I can do is to outline the choices and provide you with the facts, and, if you will permit me, to make a recommendation.

The fact is that the more expensive casket is well worth every penny you can put into it. It is what the loved one would want if he felt you were willing to get it for him.

And now I am going to tell you something that will probably surprise you. You probably think, Mr. Mixon is in the casket-selling business and it's to his interest to sell me the most expensive casket he can; it's to his interest to run down the products of his competitors and the services of other businessmen, it's to his interest to make a sale. Well, I guess that's one way of doing things and I know lots of businessmen feel that way and operate that way. So you will probably be, as I say, somewhat surprised to hear me put in a good word for those other businessmen and to hear me say that they have a right to try to do the best selling job they can, if that's all they care about.

But let me say very seriously, and with a sincere spontaneous gesture of the right hand at this point, that they do not have the right to sell you something you don't need. They do not have a right to take advantage of you in your hour of grief; they do not have a right to oversell you on groceries or medicines or anything else. Nor do I.

And so I am recommending to you, not the twenty-thousand-dollar casket, much as I would like the extra two-dollar commission; not even the nineteen-thousand-dollar casket with the gold handles, which most people would consider the indispensable minimum in marking a decent respect for the departed. I will sell you those if you want to show you really care about a loved one. But if you do not really want to do that much, I am recommending then that you take the simple eighteen-thousand-dollar casket with plastic handles.

Now, you are probably wondering why I am doing this—why I am willing to forgo the extra income that I could be making. The other day a little old lady asked me, "Mr. Mixon, sir, why is it you are willing to sell me the simple eighteen-thousand-dollar casket instead of trying to make money on me, like other businessmen, of whom you always speak so fairly, even though they try to knock you and never seem to think about anything except themselves and what's in it for them?" I will give you the same straightforward answer I gave that little old lady, even though my competitors have tried to frighten me, and my associates have warned me that such plain candor and forthrightness is dangerous and can lose me untold amounts of money. I guess it's just the way I'm built that I can't help being forthright, whatever it costs me. The reason I'm willing to sell you the eighteen-thousand-dollar casket is because making a big sale it not everything to me.

Oh, sure, I'm in business to try to sell, and my kids can use the extra milk and bread that some extra money might bring home, just the same as other folks' kids. But to me, as I unfold my hands and lean forward still more sincerely here, selling caskets involves something more than just what's best for me. I'm interested in what's best for *you*. I'm interested in casket selling as a way of life. I'm interested in caskets for every man, woman and child in this wonderful free country of ours.

And so that's why I feel the decision must be up to you, and, whatever you decide, I'll abide by it—because you're the person I want to serve. If the eighteen-thousand-dollar casket represents all that you care, if your conscience tells you that this is all you want to spend on your loved one, then you're the one who is going to live with that conscience, and, make no mistake about it, Mr. Mixon is not going to reproach you for any decision you think you can live with.

As I hand you the pen and the papers and smile at you, you can see that I am a warm and human and relaxed person, though still with all the dignity befitting a casket salesman. And I want you to be relaxed, too. So let me add that even though my forehead is a little higher than it used to be, I can still beat my competitors by a hair. I know you will not misunderstand this levity because I have used it very successfully this year, and it is altogether fitting and proper that I should do this. And so, as I smile again and raise both my hands in this completely outgoing gesture, you can see that I have left no stone unturned to be friendly; and I have not taken care of my teeth or spent that nineteen minutes a day under a sun lamp just for my health. I have done it for my work—not to serve myself, but so that I can better serve *you*. And if my eyes seem to keep shifting, it is only because I am constantly alert to your interests.

And now that you have signed the paper indicating the casket of your choice, let me say one thing more which may surprise you. There is a favor *you* can do for *me*. Soon you'll be seeing the butcher and the baker and all the other people doing business in this town—as they certainly have a right to do business, unethical though their methods may be. They may say at the funeral, Why, this looks like a pretty plain eighteen or nineteen-thousand-dollar casket. Well, just look them in the eye and say, Rick Mixon thought it was all right, if it was all I wanted to spend. And tell them this for me: Rick Mixon wants you other businessmen to know that he's your friend, that he respects you, that he understands you, even though you're out for every dirty penny you can get. Tell them, Rick Mixon doesn't do business your way, but he's big enough to understand your way of doing business. However cheap and lousy you other businessmen are, Rick Mixon is charitable enough to want to do the right thing by you. Tell them I said, Whatever disagreements Rick Mixon may have with you fellows now or in the past, when the hour of grief comes to you or yours, generous, charitable Rick Mixon will be waiting to put each one of you in the finest casket he can sell.

Thank you, madam, and good night.

**"AND HOW IS OUR LITTLE
PATIENT TODAY?"**
November 8, 1964

"HELLO—ANYFACE TO OLDFACE—I THINK WE HAVE THE ENEMY SURROUNDED"

August 28, 1966

"DON'T WORRY. THEY COULDN'T BE DOING IT TO US AGAIN"

August 7, 1966

"I'M AFRAID TO LOOK"

December 27, 1967

The Nixon "comeback" in 1968 astonished many. What was more surprising to me was the lack of any real opposition within his party. As Nixon put it, when one Republican candidate after another decided against entering the primaries, this seemed to be "the year of the dropouts." It was.

Gov. Nelson Rockefeller waffled and wavered and decided not to run—then decided he *would* run—by running a series of last-minute newspaper ads.

The Democratic presidential candidate, Hubert Humphrey, doggedly maintained that the people of the United States were not ready to put Richard Nixon in the White House. Although the people may not have been enthusiastic about Nixon, there was at least a generation which knew the Vietnam war better than it knew or remembered the "old" Nixon, and which feared minority groups and "crime in the streets" more than it feared an assault on our system of government.

Given the circumstances of the assassinations of American political leaders in the 1960s, the continuing war, and the regime of Gen. Thieu, the odds were on Nixon to win in 1968.

He fudged the war issue to keep the support of both

1968 HANDICAP EVENT
January 11, 1968

"WHAT YOU NEED IS SOMETHING NEW, LIKE THIS"
February 2, 1968

"EVERYTHING'S COMING UP ROSES"

March 24, 1968

"hawks" and "doves."

He hit hard on the "crime issue" and at the Johnson administration for not advocating wiretapping and electronic surveillance. He also attacked Supreme Court decisions which protected the rights of accused persons—calling this a strengthening of the "crime forces" against the "peace forces." He scoffed at the idea of poverty having a significant connection with crime. He declared that "a society that is lenient and permissive for criminals is a society that is neither safe nor secure for innocent men and women." Within the next few years Americans would learn of crimes that indeed were not connected with poverty, but toward which the highest government official was at least "permissive."

After the disclosures of the 1972 Nixon campaign "dirty tricks," people could only speculate on what similar activities may have taken place in 1968. There were plenty of genuine

NEW RECRUIT
May 12, 1968

September 13, 1968

**"RIGHT, GEORGE—THE STREETS
OF THIS CITY AREN'T SAFE'**

October 1, 1968

**"COME OUT, COME OUT,
WHOEVER YOU ARE!"**

September 18, 1968

protestors and angry policemen in encounters like those that occurred during the Chicago Democratic convention. We don't know whether such confrontations, there and elsewhere, were encouraged or touched off by political manipulators. We do know that they played into Nixon's hands.

He promised that if elected, he would remove Attorney General Ramsey Clark. Since a new President customarily brings in Cabinet members of his own party, this "promise" was only a slur on an incumbent.

Nixon gave the United States not only a new Attorney General but several. His first was John Mitchell, who was later indicted, acquitted, and then indicted again on other counts. Nixon's second Attorney General was Richard Kleindienst, who later pleaded guilty to a criminal offense. His next was Elliot Richardson, who—along with deputy Attorney General William Ruckelshaus—left the government in the "Saturday Night Massacre." Robert Bork then served as acting Attorney General. Nixon's last Attorney General was William Saxbe. In a twenty-two month period, between 1972 and 1974, we had no less than five chief law enforcement officers.

"Law-and-order" candidate Nixon issued a 1968 position paper on crime titled *Toward Freedom from Fear*. There was

"I DON'T GET INVOLVED IN SENATE MATTERS LIKE SUPREME COURT APPOINTMENTS"
October 3, 1968

"I DIDN'T THINK HE'D SHOOT BACK"
October 17, 1968

a little irony here, since the phrase came from one of the "four freedoms" listed by Franklin Roosevelt in opposing authoritarian governments which tapped and bugged private citizens and entered homes without warrants. The Nixon paper contained these words:

> One of the operative principles of a free society is that men are accountable for what they do. . . .
> In the preamble of the Constitution of the United States, this country set it as a goal to "establish justice" in these states. Just as justice dictates that innocent men go free, it also means that guilty men pay the penalty for their crimes. It is that second part of justice to which the nation must begin to address itself in earnest.

After Nixon left office in 1974, many of his supporters decided this "second part of justice" could be skipped. But that was five and a half years in the future. In 1968, they

THE APT PUPIL
September 11, 1968

cheered the stern words on crime of candidate Nixon. Some of them were later heartened by the tough talk and no-nonsense, no-knock policies of President Nixon—even though violent crime rose during his administration.

Equally tough was vice presidential candidate Spiro T. Agnew. In October, 1968, *The New York Times* ran some articles and editorials which called attention to his questionable record in Maryland politics and found him unfit for the Number 2 spot. But this was condemned by Nixon as a campaign smear.

Nixon, who would later profit politically as a result of "the Eagleton affair," seemed to demonstrate little concern about the record of the man he chose to be his Vice President. Speaking of Agnew, Nixon said, "The guy has got it, or he doesn't. . . . If he doesn't, then Nixon has made a bum choice." And: "You can look him in the eye and you say 'He's got it.' " As the 1968 election approached, Nixon and Agnew were leading in the polls.

When the election result seemed inevitable, Art Buchwald mentioned to me one day that this outcome ought to be good for us in our respective fields. I told him seriously that I was

**"SLUMS ARE FOR YOU
COPS TO GO INTO"**
October 20, 1968

FACING THE CRISIS
April 23, 1968

really worried about such an administration. To this he responded completely deadpan, "Herb, you've got to stop putting the country ahead of your work."

He knew that I was not looking for this kind of cartoon "material." But many people have always assumed that I viewed Nixon as a cartoonist's dream.

After the 1960 election, some perfectly pleasant people offered condolences on the "loss" of this political figure, not quite understanding that I would be happy to do without that familiar face and all it stood for. I still remember with gratitude the lady at a party who listened as guests "consoled" me, and who then pointedly asked one of them, "Why do you suppose he drew those cartoons about Nixon in the first place?"

Far from thinking of the Nixon election as a kind of cartoon bonanza, my feeling on listening to the 1968 returns was that of a person sentenced to a four-to-eight-year term. I even thought: How old will I be when I get out?—which is to say, when he leaves office.

The lines of John Adams, carved over a mantelpiece in the White House, end with the words, "May none but honest and wise men ever rule under this roof."

**"IT'S OKAY TO COME OUT
NOW—WE JUST TORE DOWN
THE RING"**
October 11, 1968

"AIN'T HE THE ONE?"
October 23, 1968

I hoped that perhaps, after all, the White House somehow did have an ennobling effect on its occupants, and that the new man in it would really become a "new Nixon."

During Eisenhower's eight years in the White House, we lived with the possibility of Nixon becoming President—and then we went through the 1960 cliffhanger election, when he almost made it.

In 1970 a strange little joke went around about a lady who had gone into a state of suspended animation ten years before. When her doctor finally brought her back to consciousness, she lifted her head, opened her eyes, and asked, "How is President Eisenhower?" The doctor replied, "Eisenhower is dead." "My God," she said, closing her eyes and falling back, "Then Nixon is President." ∎

"MIND YOU, I DON'T BELIEVE THIS SIGN WHICH SOMEONE OR OTHER PUT INTO MY HANDS"
October 27, 1968

"WE WERE BUSY MAKING SPEECHES ON LAW AND ORDER"
November 5, 1968

IN THE
WHITE HOUSE

During much of his career, I had pictured the Nixon face with "five o'clock shadow."

For the record, it should be noted that he had (and undoubtedly still has) a heavy "beard." (See photo.) Sen. Joseph McCarthy had one too. But I wouldn't have pictured it if it had not seemed to me to fit what I considered to be their political thuggery.

Some time before the 1968 Republican convention, J. R. Wiggins, who was then editor of *The Washington Post,* presented me with a brand-new razor in a handsome case, accompanied by a poem, which began:

> The neat device we here enclose
> We hereby wish to say
> (Upon the best authority)
> Is wielded twice a day
> To cut the beard you still depict
> As harvested each week

In ev'ry picture that you make
Of Nixon's chin and cheek.

The closing lines were:

The prophets say that he may win,
Perhaps by just a whisker,
And if he does, you will be blamed,
So kindly think of this, cur,
And join the good and kind and true
The faithful, just and brave,
And grasp this razor in your hand,
And give that man a shave.

                                        jrw

In replying, I wrote a couple of couplets:

Poem, like razor, is a Gem
To gladden Rep. or Ind. or Dem.
                Anon (*probably 1968*)

He's shaved with new Gillettes 'n' Schicks 'n'
Still he is the same old Nix'n.
                Ibid. (*later that day*)

I did not "give that man" a shave at the time. But after the votes were counted in November, I gave one to the President-elect.

Later in his administration, much of the mail I received asked: "Isn't it time to put the beard back on?"

Actually, Nixon did succeed in altering his physical image —to a certain extent. In addition to getting rid of his vest and hat (àla Kennedy) he also acquired something resembling a Kennedy tan. Whether from sun lamps or time in Florida and California, or augmented by make-up for the cameras, his face took on an over-all complexion which cut down on the appearance of "shadow."

Anyhow, the barbershop drawing, later identified by *Time* magazine as my "honeymoon cartoon," was recognized for what it was: a chance for the new President to start fresh.

November 7, 1968

"DOWN THE CHIMNEY DICK NIXOLAS CAME WITH A BOUND"
December 10, 1968

POST-INAUGURAL PARADE

January 21, 1969

January 23, 1969

February 14, 1969

**"HAS HE HEARD THAT YOU'RE
AGAINST INFLATION?"**

March 28, 1969

Following that, I did a kind of tease routine in the drawings, showing Nixon a couple of times in outfits that concealed the lower part of his face, until his inauguration—when the "new" face appeared.

In publicly disclosing and introducing all his Cabinet selections at one time, via one of his televised "firsts," Nixon told the wives of the new Cabinet members that they would have to get used to seeing their husbands caricatured in my cartoons.

The first of the Cabinet I had occasion to do was Secretary of the Interior Walter Hickel, who was not confirmed by the Senate until after the rest of the Cabinet had been sworn in. I depicted him as still putting on his pants while joining the new administration as it marched forward. When he was confirmed, he said in a broadcast that I would be glad to know he had now gotten his pants on.

The tone of the early cartoons was also good-natured, though they could not remain for months entirely uncritical without ignoring the policies of the new administration and abandoning the role of the cartoonist.

The March 28 cartoon of Secretary of Defense Melvin

"AS SOON AS MIRV IS READY, HE'LL GO TO THE CONFERENCE WITH YOU"

July 1, 1969

"AH, BUT ONCE HE'S PAID HIS DEBTS TO THURMOND, DIRKSEN, TOWER, GOLDWATER . . ."

July 11, 1969

"SORRY—WE'RE FEEDING
ALL THE MOUTHS WE CAN"
May 2, 1969

"TAKE THAT—AND THAT!—"
June 5, 1969

"ACTUALLY, DR. KNOWLES, I WAS
CALLING ABOUT SOME
TROUBLE I'VE BEEN HAVING
WITH MY BACK"
June 29, 1969

"YOU CAN SEE WHY WE HAD TO
HAVE TWO WHITE HOUSES"
August 29, 1969

Laird was an example of one in which the President was shown as an onlooker.

Nixon's apparent failure to follow up quickly on President Johnson's moves toward arms limitation concerned me. But I was concerned in another way about an "old Nixon" technique pictured in the boxing-match cartoon of June 5. This was the setting up of straw men to represent what his critics supposedly advocated. I didn't know of any responsible people who really wanted to make America weak, or end America's influence as a great power.

The later "SALT" agreements reached with Russia in 1972 (and announced after a much-televised trip) were hopeful. But the basic problem of restraining MIRV (the hydra-headed, many-nuclear-bombs-in-one vehicle) was still with us even after the Nixon return trip to Moscow in June, 1974.

In less than half a year of the Nixon administration, it was becoming clear that there was no priority on the needs of the poor, of school children, of minorities, of those without clout.

**"UNFORTUNATELY, SOME . . .
WILL FEEL THIS NECESSARY
ADJUSTMENT MORE
DIRECTLY THAN OTHERS"**
October 19, 1969

**"YOU HAVE JUST HEARD
A SPEECH BY THE PRESIDENT OF
THE UNITED STATES . . ."**
November 16, 1969

**"NEVER MIND WHY—JUST GET
RID OF ALL THOSE STUPID
BALLOON PICTURES"**

January 21, 1970

MATH LESSON

January 27, 1970

**"AND PUT IN A
HIGHER FENCE TOO"**

June 17, 1970

**"YOU HAVE JUST HEARD THE
PRESIDENT OF THE UNITED
STATES. PLEASE STAY
TUNED FOR THE
CLARIFYING STATEMENTS"**

August 7, 1970

The "Housing Notes" cartoon of January 8, 1970, makes the first reference to the cost to taxpayers of the Nixon properties—in contrast to a neglected national need. The amounts becoming known then seem modest indeed in comparison with what we learned later.

One difference between the homes of this President and those of other Presidents was apparent early.

Franklin Roosevelt had the family home at Hyde Park, where he was born and raised. Long before he became President, Truman had a modest house in Independence, Missouri. Eisenhower, who spent his life in the Army, acquired his Gettysburg retreat, not far from Washington, after becoming President. There was the well-known Kennedy family compound at Hyannisport. And Johnson had long owned his ranch.

But Nixon acquired two properties, one in Florida and the other in California, within months after the counting of the

HOUSING NOTES FROM ALL OVER
January 8, 1970

**"LISTEN, THERE'S NOTHING
WRONG WITH THIS JUDGE
EXCEPT HIS JUDGEMENT"**

November 19, 1969

**"THEY'RE THINKING OF RENAMIN
IT THE MASON-NIXON LINE"**

April 12, 19.

**"I DON'T SMELL ANYTHING—I
DON'T SMELL ANYTHING—I
DON'T SMELL ANYTHING—
I DON'T—WHEW—"**

March 11, 1970

**"DON'T BE SUCH A STRICT
CONSTRUCTIONIST"**

January 23, 197(

election returns that would put him in the White House for four years. These acquisitions were at least an unusual way to begin a presidency.

In gaining that office, Nixon had followed the Goldwater plan of "southern strategy." But what originally seemed to be a campaign device to woo the Strom Thurmonds and John Towers was becoming administration policy. It was shaping up as a "middle" position between desegregation-after-fifteen-years and segregation-forever. The "faithful execution of the laws" did not apply strictly to desegregation or to the voting rights acts, through which blacks had become enfranchised in the South.

Such policies had much to do with the way people perceived the relationship between this President and Congress.

It was argued that many of the same "liberals" who used to want a "strong President" reversed themselves in the case of Nixon and wanted to "weaken the presidency." Most of this was a playing with words. Nobody argued for Presidents to flout the law of the land. The desire for "strong Presidents" was for Presidents strong in their support of civil rights, civil liberties, and the welfare of the disadvantaged— as against Congresses largely dominated by nonrepresenta-

SECOND FRONT

April 2, 1970

"TUT TUT—THEY'RE JUST MEDIOCRE DECEPTIONS"

March 31, 1970

**"RELAX, BOY—WE AIN'T GONNA
LET NOBODY INVESTIGATE
YOU BUT US"**

March 13, 1970

**"I THOUGHT HE WAS SUPPOSED
TO GROW IN THE JOB"**

April 10, 1970

**"THAT TERRIBLE CONGRESS
—LOOK AT ALL THE THINGS
THEY DIDN'T APPROVE"**

January 8, 1971

**"IT'S SUCH A GOOD DEAL YOU'VE
GOT TO SIGN QUICK—AND DON'T
KICK THE TIRES ON THIS ONE"**

December 7, 1971

On July 24th, 1971, Nixon said to John D.
Ehrlichman, "Nobody follows up on a god-
damned thing. You remember the meeting we
had when I told that group of clowns we had
around here, Renchburg and that group. What's
his name?" Ehrlichman replied, "Rehnquist."

Three months later, in nominating Rehnquist
and Powell to the Supreme Court, Nixon said,
"These are names you will remember, because
they will add distinction and excellence in the
highest degree to the Supreme Court. . . ."

tive committee chairmen who showed little enthusiasm for these principles of democracy in practice.

Thanks partly to the Supreme Court's one-man, one-vote decision, Congress is more representative than it used to be. And while the seniority system has not been seriously threatened, fewer committees are dominated by old-line Dixie autocrats.

But Nixon found natural allies in the most regressive members of Congress. One of these was James O. Eastland (D-Miss.), chairman of the Senate Judiciary Committee, who was brought to his powerful position by seniority.

What Nixon did was to combine the worst features of the "imperial presidency" with the worst features of the congressional feudal system.

In nominating G. Harrold Carswell for a place on the Supreme Court, in 1970, Nixon followed his southern strategy with a vengeance. Carswell was not merely "mediocre," to use the word of one of his defenders. He had made a white supremacy speech in 1948; and after the Supreme Court desegregation decision, he took part in converting a public golf course into a private club. He also managed to make misstatements to the senators at his confirmation hearings. Later

"WE HAVE A NO-KNOCK POLICY FOR THAT TOO—WE DON'T KNOCK IT"

August 25, 1970

"LOOK AT THIS, BOY—SEE HOW WE'RE PROTECTING YOU?"

August 28, 1970

**"IT'S A LIBEL FOR ANYONE
TO SUGGEST THERE MIGHT
BE LIMITS TO HOW FAR YOU CAN
GO IN 1972"**

September 19, 1971

**"WHAT DO YOU MEAN, TRY IT ON
OUR TOP OFFICIALS? THAT
WOULD BE INSULTING!"**

September 8, 1971

**"YOU CAN SEE AT A QUICK
GLANCE THAT THINGS ARE
PICKING UP"**

October 28, 1970

**NEW FIGURE ON THE
AMERICAN SCENE**

June 20, 1971

that year he was defeated for the Republican nomination for U.S. senator from Florida—repudiated by his fellow party members in his own state.

Nixon had described opposition to his previous unsuccessful nomination of Clement Haynsworth to the Supreme Court as "vicious character assassination." He now used the Carswell rejection by the Senate as an excuse for another demagogic attack, accusing that body of having an obvious prejudice against a southerner on the Court. To many observers, these attacks marked a low point in his presidential politicking up to that point.

The "old" Nixon was even more in evidence in the 1970 off-year congressional elections, when he waged an ugly campaign directed against student "bums" and other dissenters.

Aiding in the campaign was Vice President Spiro T. Ag-

"OH—AND TO YOU DOWN THERE, WARM REGARDS"

April 27, 1971

**"I'M GLAD TO SEE NIXON'S
AGAINST KIDS WHO THROW
ROCKS AND TALK DIRTY"**
October 20, 1970

**"THEY'RE WILLING TO GET
ALONG WITH ANYONE BUT ME"**
July 21, 1971

**"ALL YOU KIDS KNOW ARE
FOUR-LETTER OBSCENITIES"**
September 18, 1970

**"LADIES AND GENTLEMEN—TH
PRESIDENT OF VARIOUS
SECTIONS OF THE
UNITED STATES"**
May 27, 197

new, who had previously served as the "cutting edge" in the attacks on the press. Agnew now followed the President's line in conducting a low-level attack on "effete snobs" and "radiclibs" (for radical liberals), who did not support Nixon and his policies. This campaign occasioned a third "sewer cartoon," with Nixon now showing Agnew the route.

The voters were not turned on by this campaigning, and the Democrats not only retained both houses of Congress, but gained several governorships as well.

The post-election golf-score cartoon—based on Nixon's many explanations of the election losses—brought a couple of phone calls from the White House requesting the original for Nixon. I explained that the drawings are all saved (which they have been for years), and did not volunteer a reproduction instead. I don't know what kind of inscription I could have written to this President. I also don't know why this cartoon brought those requests. Perhaps it was because the drawing showed Nixon in a sports outfit; possibly it was because an effort was being made to rehabilitate the "new Nixon" after the reversion to the "old Nixon" in the campaign and the attacks on the press. I was relieved that there were no further requests on behalf of President Nixon. ■

"NOW, WHEN YOU GET TO THIS CITY YOU TURN RIGHT AND COME UP AT THE AUDITORIUM"
October 11, 1970

"NOW, ON THE HOLE BEFORE THAT ONE—WHEN YOU CONSIDER THE WIND AND THE CONDITION OF THE FAIRWAY AND WHERE THEY PLACED THE PIN . . ."
November 15, 1970

THE NEW SECURITY
February 14, 1971

"THAT'S NOT EXACTLY THE KIND OF REVENUE SHARING WE HAD IN MIND"
March 4, 1971

"IT'S FOR SECURITY—IT MAKES US FEEL MORE SECURE"
March 14, 1971

BREAKING SCANDALS

The first of the Nixon administration scandals to appear in my cartoons dealt with the Milk Fund in September, 1971. This was more than eight months before the Watergate break-in. But that was when the scandals began for some of us. Newspaper stories told of the sudden reversal of administration policy on milk price supports, when milk producers' contributions started flowing into dummy Nixon committees —shortly after a White House meeting between Nixon and the milk producers.

1971

On March 22, 1971, ten days after it was announced that there would be *no* increased price supports, the milk producers' contributions began.

On March 23, the producers met with Nixon.

On March 24, the price support increase was announced.

This seemed to me a palpable scandal—even before we learned that the "milk contribution" offer came to $2 million and that the White House timing of the price boost was carefully calculated. My concern apparently was not shared by most members of Congress.

I don't go in for lobbying with politicians. Those who are

MILK RUN

September 29, 1971

interested in what I think can generally find out easily enough. Also, I don't think dinner parties are the place to discuss politics with public figures, unless they indicate that this is what they want to talk about—which they often do.

But the Nixon Milk Fund—with all its dummy committees and with the direct involvement of the President—seemed to me so outrageous that I found myself taking congressmen aside at parties to offer them my views about it. The interest they evinced was polite but not serious: "Please drop me a line on that, will you?" "Would you send me those clippings?" One Democratic congressman patiently explained to me that the Milk Fund was not important, "because corruption will not be an issue in 1972." Well, it certainly wouldn't be unless people cared enough to speak up about it. Ralph Nader did—in a lawsuit filed on behalf of the public.

One member of Congress who did share my feelings about the Milk Fund and volunteered that I was on the right track was Thomas P. (Tip) O'Neill Jr. (D.-Mass.)—then House majority whip. He also understood—sooner than most of his

"THINK OF YOURSELF AS CONTRIBUTING TO 'THE NEW PROSPERITY' "
November 25, 1971

December 1, 1971

**"CALL MRS. BEARD'S DOCTOR
—THERE'S BEEN A
TERRIBLE ACCIDENT"**

March 22, 1972

"DOWN, DAMMIT!"

March 28, 1972

**"HOW WOULD YOU LIKE TO SEE
SOME HOT PICTURES INSTEAD?"**

April 4, 1972

**"TELL THE HOUSEWIVES WE ARE
CONTINUING OUR FIGHT
AGAINST INFLATION"**

March 31, 1972

colleagues—that Nixon & Co. played a type of hardball politics unlike anything we had seen before.

In the spring of 1972, the nation learned of ITT's offer of hundreds of thousands of dollars (the general estimate was $400,000) toward financing the Republican convention which was to be held in San Diego. Some time after the story broke, Nixon changed the scheduled convention site to Miami Beach.

San Diego had other unpleasant connotations. Deputy Attorney General Richard Kleindienst and Assistant Attorney General Henry E. Petersen had helped sweep under the rug misconduct by the U.S. Attorney in San Diego, Harry Steward. Steward had quashed a grand jury subpoena against one Nixon fund raiser and quashed an investigation of another Nixon friend for conspiring to violate federal tax laws and the Corrupt Practices Act.

It turned out that Kleindienst had also been offered a bribe —but he did not think to report it to the FBI until he learned that the man who offered the bribe was about to be put under electronic surveillance by the FBI.

While ITT was making its generous political financial offer, the administration was being generous in dropping anti-trust

TANGLED WEB
April 7, 1972

"A FUNNY THING HAPPENED ON THE WAY BACK FROM THE BARBECUE. I RAN INTO SOME DAMN DEMOCRATS IN A PRIMARY—"
May 12, 1972

"ISN'T THERE SOME SIMPLE WORD FOR ALL THAT?"

April 13, 1972

"I DO SOLEMNLY REFRESH MY MEMORY AND TRY TO RECALL TO THE BEST OF MY ABILITY . . ."

June 2, 1972

"IT'S STILL THERE"

June 11, 1972

TIP OF THE ICEBERG

June 13, 1972

suits against ITT. Later, ITT found it expedient to run a lot of memos through a shredding machine. (We subsequently learned that after the Watergate break-in Nixon aides also made hasty use of shredding machines.)

Shortly after the ITT disclosures, Kleindienst was nominated to succeed John Mitchell as Attorney General of the United States. In the course of the Senate confirmation hearings, Kleindienst, who was under oath, said that the ITT anti-trust suit had been handled exclusively by the former anti-trust chief, Richard McLaren. This turned out to be untrue. He also stated flatly that no pressure had been put upon him by higher officials to settle the suits—a statement later shown to be untrue with the disclosure of an April 1971, Nixon phone call to him.

Nixon said, after brief preliminary words: "I want something clearly understood, and, if it is not understood, McLaren's ass is to be out within one hour. The IT & T thing— stay the hell out of it. Is that clear? That's an order."

Kleindienst asked: "Well you mean the order is to—"

Nixon then interrupted to say: "The order is to leave the God damned thing alone."

In 1974, Kleindienst—by then a former Attorney General of the United States—pleaded guilty to a charge that he failed to testify "accurately and fully"—a euphemistic description of his offense, but one that avoided the use of the word perjury, which would have made it a felony case.

Following a number of cartoons on Kleindienst, ITT, and secret Nixon funds, I did the June 13, 1972, Tip Of The Iceberg cartoon.

Four days later an incident occurred which would ultimately result in some disclosures of the depth of that iceberg, and of corruption and scandals previously unknown in the Nixon administration—or any other administration in American history.

At 2:00 A.M. Saturday morning, June 17, five men—wearing surgical rubber gloves—were apprehended while burgling the offices of the Democratic National Committee in one of the Watergate buildings.

**"WHO WOULD THINK OF DOING
SUCH A THING?"**

June 20, 1972

**"REMEMBER, WE DON'T TALK
TILL WE GET A LAWYER"**

June 21, 1972

The first cartoon I did following the Saturday break-in was drawn on Monday for the following day's paper (June 20): "Who Would Think Of Doing Such A Thing?" On the basis of what we already knew about Nixon and his two Attorneys General—who believed in bugging, tapping, "no-knock" entry, and practically unlimited presidential powers—it was hardly jumping to conclusions to figure people might very easily do such a thing in the climate created by these leaders. They might well do such a thing on behalf of such leadership, or even with the knowledge or general approval of such leadership. And by Monday it was already known that one of the burglars was on at least one Nixon re-election payroll.

The following day, the same three administration officials appear in the cartoon, "Remember, We Don't Talk Till We Get A Lawyer."

I recall early in the administration how Nixon kept reminding us that he was a lawyer. And in introducing some of his appointees, he boasted that this or that one was a "lawyer's lawyer." It was later interesting to see, in that law-and-order administration, how many of those "lawyers' lawyers" needed *lawyers' lawyers' lawyers* to keep them out of jail.

The cartoon two days later showed the footprints leading into the White House.

At this point a word is in order about Watergate—the name of a group of apartment and office buildings in Washington, D.C. The name Watergate has become a generic term for Nixon administration corruption and crimes. This is unfortunate, because so many people associate the word only with the crime that took place in one building one night.

Nixon took advantage of that confusion to talk about Watergate (and his involvement) as if on the basis of the burglary alone. When the House Judiciary Committee was holding its impeachment inquiry, Nixon lawyer James St. Clair tried to set narrow limits to the scope of the House inquiry by protesting that Watergate is "the name of the game."

The name of what it was all about was the faithful execution of the laws of the United States. And it was not a game except to those who did not mind playing games with the American people.

The cases of the Milk Fund, ITT, and the Department of Justice show that the corruption associated with Nixon did not begin with Watergate. And it did not end there.

What the Watergate building doors opened onto was not just a few burglars at work but a whole vast array of Nixon administration crimes.

Those doors, with the taped locks, were like the "Open, Sesame!" that brought an amazed Ali Baba into the cave of the forty thieves.

These thieves tried to steal the United States Government. ■

"STRANGE—THEY ALL SEEM TO HAVE SOME CONNECTION WITH THIS PLACE"

June 23, 1972

CRACKS IN THE DAM

A couple of days after the Watergate break-in, the White House press secretary dismissed it as "a third-rate burglary."

In succeeding weeks and months, when administration officials referred to it at all, it was as an isolated incident. They called it the "Watergate caper"—a term which became widely used in the press and on television. Vice President Agnew even suggested that the break-in at Democratic head-quarters might have been committed by Democrats in an ef-fort to cast blame on Nixon campaigners. But according to a former White House aide, Jeb Stuart Magruder, Agnew already knew this was not so.

As the spreading scandals unfolded in a few newspapers —most notably The Washington Post—President Nixon de-clared there had been no White House involvement in Wa-tergate, and his press secretary, Ronald Ziegler, denounced the Post's disclosures as "the shoddiest kind of journalism."

In August, Nixon was referring to Watergate as a "very bizarre incident." Nine months later—in the spring of 1973

**"THE SECRET NEGOTIATIONS
ABROAD ARE NOTHING
COMPARED TO THE ONES
AT HOME"**

August 3, 1972

**"I'D LIKE TO TAKE YOUR
RUBBER-GLOVE PRINTS, PLEASE"**

August 11, 1972

**". . . OUR PRESIDENT, WHOSE
BOLD LEADERSHIP IS ALREADY
BEGINNING TO BRING US OUT OF
THE NIXON RECESSION . . ."**

August 16, 1972

**"IT WAS A GREAT CONVENTION,
IT WAS A GREAT CONVENTION, IT
WAS A . . ."**

August 24, 1972

—he was calling it a "very deplorable incident." Almost a year after the break-in, when the scandals continued to grow despite efforts of containment, he was retroactively "appalled" by the Watergate break-in.

The cartoon of Nixon saying, "Keep The Lid On Till After The Election!" appeared on the morning of August 29.

In a news conference that day Nixon explained that a special prosecutor would not "serve any useful purpose." He said, ". . . we are doing everything we can to take this incident and to investigate it and not to cover it up. . . . What really hurts in matters of this sort . . . is if you try to cover it up."

In the same press conference he made a couple of other noteworthy statements.

One was that an investigation had cleared all those currently employed in his administration of complicity in Watergate.

Another had to do with the direction of the Nixon re-election campaign, then at its height. Nixon had always said that he ran his own political campaigns and seemed to reaffirm this

"ANYONE WHO THOUGHT WE WERE BLOWING A CHANCE FOR PEACE SHOULD HAVE SPOKEN UP"

August 15, 1972

"KEEP THE LID ON TILL AFTER THE ELECTION!"

August 29, 1972

**"IT'S—UH—SORT OF A GOOD
NEIGHBOR POLICY"**

August 31, 1972

"STOP THE MUSIC!"

September 3, 1972

**THE DARK AT THE TOP
OF THE STAIRS**

August 25, 1972

"THERE'S NO NEED FOR AN INDEPENDENT INVESTIGATION— WE HAVE EVERYTHING WELL IN HAND"

September 8, 1972

GOLDEN HARVEST

September 13, 1972

"YOU SURE THAT'S THE SWEET SMELL OF SUCCESS?"

September 14, 1972

**"IT'S NOT QUITE THE WAY
I HOPED HE'D GROW IN THE JOB"**

September 20, 1972

**"CONFIDENTIALLY, JUST
BETWEEN US DEMOCRATS
—AND OF COURSE, YOU, MR.
COLSON, AND YOU, MR. STANS,
AND YOU, MR. NIXON. . ."**

September 15, 1972

**"NOW PUT IN CALLS TO MUSKIE,
McGOVERN, HUMPHREY
AND LINDSAY—"**

January 5, 1972

in answering a question about the current race.

He said: "I am conducting this campaign, and I have urged on my colleagues in the campaign to conduct it without regard to the polls."

This statement was made only a little more than two months before the 1972 election.

The following year, when the scandals, the cover-ups, and the subversion of the electoral process could no longer be contained, Nixon said that he had *not* run the 1972 campaign. This, he said, was because he had been too busy running the affairs of the nation, and particularly its foreign policy.

But the August 29, 1972, statement came months after the trips to China and Russia. Even the planning for those events had not preoccupied the President to a point where he was too busy to phone in suggestions to football teams—or to call signals for his own political team.

Much of what Nixon's team was doing was learned from the newspapers, which kept turning up surprising facts during that campaign.

Between June 17 and the November 7 election, some publications and some commentators had told readers and listeners about quite a few things—in addition to the ITT scandal, the Milk Fund, and the Watergate break-in itself:

"THIS BROADCAST PAID FOR BY . . ."

September 27, 1972

"WELL, WHAT THE HELL—MAYBE A FEW MORE—"

September 28, 1972

"THERE YOU ARE, BOY—
NICE BONE—"

September 17, 1972

The bloodhound in this cartoon bears a similarity to the one that began dogging Nixon after his "Checkers" speech. This time he stayed on the trail.

"OUR STATISTICS SHOW THAT
THINGS ARE BETTER THAN THEY
WOULD BE IF THEY WERE WORSE
THAN THEY ARE"

September 29, 1972

"IT'S GLOBAL DIPLOMACY
AND HIGH FINANCE.
YOU WOULDN'T
UNDERSTAND. PAY HERE"

October 8, 1972

"GOODNESS, ANOTHER POOR
CHAP WHO LOOKS AS IF HE MIGHT
NOT PULL THROUGH"

October 5, 1972

There was the quickie bank charter given to a Nixon fund raiser who had contributed $25,000 to the Nixon campaign —a sum that wound up in the bank account of one of the burglars.

There were the millions of dollars in secret Nixon funds.

There was the laundering of campaign money through Mexican bank accounts.

There was the destruction of evidence at the Committee for the Re-election of the President ("CREEP").

There was the fact that "CREEP" representatives sat in when the FBI interviewed "CREEP" employees.

There were the dossiers on individuals used to help solicit "voluntary" contributions from businessmen.

There was the political use of the Justice Department and the administration "investigations" which did not disclose anything.

**LATEST ITEM PULLED OUT
OF THE SWAMP**
October 1, 1972

ALL QUIET ALONG THE POTOMAC

October 4, 1972

"SORRY, MA'AM—THE LOWER LEVEL IS NOT PART OF THE WHITE HOUSE TOUR"

October 15, 1972

October 6, 1972

"THE NEWSPAPER STORIES ARE DESPICABLE—AND WE REFUSE TO ANSWER ANY QUESTIONS"

October 18, 1972

"AND THAT'S JUST THE RUG TO COVER THE WALL-TO-WALL MONEY"

October 10, 1972

"MIRACULOUS—HE CAN WALK ON MUD"

October 19, 1972

There was the disclosure that the Watergate bugging was only one incident in a massive campaign of political espionage conceived in the White House as basic re-election strategy.

There were the faked letters and other "dirty tricks" of Donald Segretti, who reported to presidential appointments secretary Dwight Chapin.

There were the hundreds of thousands of dollars kept in former Secretary of Commerce Maurice Stans' private safe.

There was the fact that Haldeman, Kalmbach, Magruder, and Attorney General John Mitchell had access to or controlled secret funds, some of which were used for espionage and sabotage.

It's a safe bet that fewer people knew about the hundreds of thousands of dollars in the Nixon campaign espionage and sabotage fund than knew about the "1000%" support Sen. George McGovern had given his running mate when he first

"TIME TO GO UPSTAIRS AND DO THE PRESIDENT-OF-ALL-THE-PEOPLE BIT"
October 22, 1972

October 13, 1972

TRUNK LINE
October 24, 1972

**"IT DOESN'T EXIST—AND
BESIDES, HE DOESN'T HAVE
ANYTHING TO DO WITH IT"**
October 26, 1972

THE GREAT SILENCE
October 31, 1972

POLLS SHOW LANDSLIDE

JUSTICE

OFFICIAL COVER-UPS

POLITICAL USE OF FBI

PAYOFFS FROM BIG INTERESTS

TAPPING AND BUGGING

ITT

SECRET FUNDS

POLITICAL ESPIONAGE AND SABOTAGE

FAKED LETTERS

SPECIAL DEALS

©1972 HERBLOCK

November 1, 1972

FRONT RUNNER
November 2, 1972

"IN THE BAG, CHIEF"
November 5, 1972

**"REMEMBER, IT ISN'T WHETHER
YOU WON OR LOST—"**
November 9, 1972

**"I'M STAYING ON FOR ANOTHER
VOYAGE—BUT FROM NOW ON, NO
MORE MR. NICE GUY!"**
November 16, 1972

heard—not from the running mate but from the press—of an Eagleton medical record that was sure to surface in the campaign. And many of those who did read or hear about the Nixon scandals were prepared to believe that they were campaign smears fostered by "the media."

Nixon's landslide re-election was trumpeted as a mandate. But even after the facts of the campaign methods used became known, few asked why—if the people wanted to give Nixon a mandate—it was necessary for him to use so much illegal money, or to employ such subversion and sabotage in manipulating the opposition party's choice of candidates. Even fewer recalled that when the White House campaign of espionage and sabotage began in 1971, the polls showed leading Democratic contender Edmund Muskie actually running ahead of Nixon.

And few asked why the Nixon "mandate" was not reflected in the congressional elections.

In November, 1972, Nixon carried forty-nine states.

He seemed invincible.

"I DIDN'T REALIZE IT APPLIED JUST TO HIM"

December 12, 1972

"YOU DON'T HAVE QUITE THE RIGHT SLANT"

December 22, 1972

**"IT SAYS THAT'S THE TV
AND PRESS SECTION"**

December 29, 1972

**"WE DON'T KNOW WHERE
WE GOT THE MONEY AND WE
DON'T KNOW WHAT PRESIDENT
WE WERE RE-ELECTING"**

January 19, 1973

PARADE

January 14, 1973

**"WE'VE DONE EVERYTHING
POSSIBLE TO GET TO THE
BOTTOM OF THIS. WE JUST DON'T
WANT ANYONE TO GET TO
THE TOP OF IT"**

February 4, 1973

**"GREAT NEWS, CHIEF! WE'VE GOT
THE CUFFS ON ONE OF JACK
ANDERSON'S MEN"**

February 7, 1973

On the arrest of Les Whitten by the FBI. The
government later dropped charges. Jack Anderson wrote that "the false arrest of my associate . . . was used as a pretext for launching a
massive FBI investigation into our operations."

**"HOW ARE YOU ON
SACRED BULLS?"**

February 2, 1973

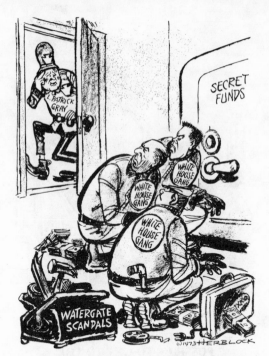

**"OOPS—SORRY—I WOULDN'T
INTRUDE ON HIGHLY
PLACED GENTLEMEN"**

March 4, 1973

SHADOWED

February 27, 1973

**"I CAN NOT TELL A LIE. I DID IT
TO MAKE THEM STRONG
AND SELF-RELIANT"**

February 18, 1973

"THE FBI NEEDS A LEADER"
—L. PATRICK GRAY

March 9, 1973

**'POLLUTION IS CLEANLINESS . . .
DECAY IS PROGRESS . . . CRIME
INCREASE IS SAFETY . . . YOU ARE
VERY VERY HAPPY . . ."**

March 7, 1973

**"I'VE DECIDED TO PUT
THEM BACK, SO LET'S JUST
FORGET THE WHOLE THING"**

March 13, 1973

THE FLOOD

Throughout the fall and winter of 1972, and the early months of 1973, Haynes Johnson of *The Washington Post*—one of the keenest political observers and best writers in American journalism—went up and down the country to learn what people were thinking. He found not only that there was no public outcry about the scandals, but that during the first few months of the press disclosures, the people he talked with did not even mention Watergate. And at the beginning of his second term, President Nixon's popularity was at a high point of 68 per cent in the polls.

On March 19, 1973, Watergate defendant James McCord wrote a letter to Judge Sirica telling of perjury, pressure to keep silent, and the involvement of higher-ups in the Watergate case.

By April, Haynes Johnson found that the public "refusal to believe it all" had given way to questions about Watergate.

It had taken the Watergate scandals ten months to get to

132

"ANYTHING YOU SAY ABOUT THESE GENTLEMEN WILL BE KEPT STRICTLY CONFIDENTIAL"
March 20, 1973

"WE DON'T CALL IT 'TAKING THE FIFTH' ANY MORE"
March 16, 1973

FIRM STAND ON CRIME
March 15, 1973

"HOW CAN ANYTHING TOUCH US AFTER OUR LANDSLIDE?"

March 25, 1973

the top of the news.

For anyone who took seriously the Nixon administration's complaints about the press, this might serve to illustrate the enormous power of the presidency in terms of influencing news and public understanding.

Most of the news from Washington is generally news of, by, and for the executive branch of government—what Cabinet members say, what press secretaries say, what "information" departments put out, what the Vice President says, what "the White House" says—and particularly what the President says. Nowhere in what we call the free world does one man have control over such vast machinery for influencing public opinion as does the chief executive of the United States. Under the Nixon administration, there were not only

March 27, 1973

... WHEN THE PIE WAS
OPENED, THE BIRDS
BEGAN TO SING ...

March 29, 1973

"WE WANT TO DISPEL THE MY"
... THAT WE
SEEK TO COVER UP."
—WHITE HOUSE

April 1, 19

HAIL TO THE CHIEF

April 5, 1973

"PITY"

April 8, 1973

expanded press staffs and White House aides, but a "communications" staff, mostly engaged in one-way communications—putting out propaganda and orchestrating attacks on critics.

In these assaults on "the media," the administration lumped together those who either opposed it or who gave out facts it didn't like. I was one of those singled out for special mention in the attacks on the press made through Agnew.

Being on Agnew's "list" brought me more congratulatory calls and letters and more envious comments from fellow journalists than a prize might have. Several who wrote me called it "the Spiro T. Agnew Award." But much of the other mail I got during this long period was not friendly. And since more than 90 per cent of the press editorially supported Nixon in 1972, I was aware that some editors were bothered that I felt it necessary to do so many cartoons on the scandals. I have a special warmth for the ones who sent me—along with some of their readers' vitriolic letters—encouraging notes like: "We're getting lots of complaints about you, but

"IT MAY NOT BE TOUCHING YOU, BOSS, BUT IT'S GETTING TO ME"
April 12, 1973

"IT'S CALLED SEPARATION OF POWERS—WE SEPARATE YOU FROM YOUR POWERS"
April 15, 1973

"... I CAN REPORT TODAY THAT THERE HAVE BEEN
MAJOR DEVELOPMENTS ..."

April 18, 1973

keep doing those cartoons."

Nixon seemed to think much of symbols and pictures as a medium for getting messages across quickly, and often showed a special concern about cartoons and photographs. He knew that finger pointed at Khrushchev would have more impact on Americans than what was said. On one occasion when he and others in the Eisenhower administration went to the airport to meet a plane from abroad, he gave the word that no one was to carry an umbrella "for obvious reasons" (the association of Neville Chamberlain's umbrella with "appeasement").

Nixon had for years made the name Yalta—the Russian city where Roosevelt, Churchill, and Stalin had met in 1945 —another synonym for appeasement or sellout. He had called for the repudiation of Yalta commitments which he said "abet the Communist slavery of nations." On one of his own trips to Russia, in the summer of 1974, President Nixon was unhappy that Soviet Premier Brezhnev had arranged a meeting at the same resort city. It was an uncomfortable

"SOMEBODY HAS TO THINK ABOUT TOMORROW"

April 27, 1973

"OH, HELLO—UH—LOOK WHAT I'M UNCOVERING HERE"

April 20, 1973

**"WE'RE NOT CONNECTED
WITH ANY NIXON FUNDS. WE'RE
JUST ON OUR WAY TO DO SOME
FOOD SHOPPING"**

April 22, 1973

**"OKAY, I'VE GOT IT FASTENED—
WHAT'S THE LATEST?"**

April 24, 1973

"YOU'RE MY BOY"

April 26, 1973

An Agnew statement supporting Nixon prompted
the "You're My Boy" cartoon—a title which
echoes Eisenhower's statement when he decided
to keep Nixon on the ticket in 1952.

April 29, 1973

Nixon who sat for pictures with the smiling Soviet leader at Yalta.

Nixon knew quite early that if one picture was worth a lot of words, many pictures in motion could be worth much more. He always gestured for the cameras as if he had been told to "do something" for a home movie. And despite his intemperate attacks on a few newscasters, he had made television work for him very effectively indeed. The Checkers broadcast in 1952 did for him what no written statement could.

In *The Selling of the President,* Joe McGinnis described how, in the 1968 campaign, Nixon did an end-run around the press by staging supposedly spontaneous question-and-answer sessions for the TV cameras. Toward the end of his

May 1, 1973

"OFFICIAL BUSINESS"

May 6, 1973

On the news that the Nixon "plumbers" had broken into the office of Dr. Fielding, who had been Daniel Ellsberg's psychiatrist.

"LAST JUNE I WAS APPALLED— BUT THEN IT SLIPPED MY MIND, OR SOMETHING"

May 2, 1973

May 3, 197

administration he returned a couple of times to the non-press conference in TV appearances before friendly groups which could even be counted on to applaud his answers to easy questions. This operation might have been called The Re-Selling of the President.

Once in the White House Nixon made the most of the networks' willingness to give a President all major channels any time he chose. After his administration's scandals became more widely reported by the media, he made a series of statements and television appearances designed to turn back the rising tide of "Watergate" problems.

On April 18, I drew the first of several cartoons showing the waters rising around the White House. The title ("I can report today that there have been major developments . . ."), came from a statement President Nixon made that day. There was speculation at the time about what particular development he had in mind—private testimony—news of what a judge or grand jury was being told—FBI reports—what?

Some fifteen months later *The Washington Post* put this statement into context by matching it up with tape transcripts. That article provides such a revealing exposition of how Nixon and his advisers worked, that it is included here in its entirety:

Nixon, Adviser Picked March 21

On April 17, 1973, President Nixon walked into the White House press briefing room and said:

"On March 21, as a result of serious charges which came to my attention, some of which were publicly reported, I began intensive new inquiries into this whole matter . . . I can report today that there have been major developments in the [Watergate] case concerning which it would be improper to be more specific now, except to say that real progress has been made in finding the truth."

Just a few minutes earlier, according to the White

**"I HAVE BEEN AUTHORIZED
TO LOOK YOU IN THE EYE AND
DENY HE DID ANYTHING"**

May 9, 1973

DISASTER AREA

May 11, 1973

**"I CAN'T UNDERSTAND HOW WE
KEEP LOSING THESE
CONSPIRACY CASES"**

May 13, 1973

**"WE DIDN'T GET TO SEE
HIM OFTEN, BUT WE CAN'T SAY
HE DIDN'T GIVE US A HEARING"**

May 17, 1973

On the news that high Nixon administration
officials had tapped the phones of its own national security advisers, and of newsmen.

House edited tape transcripts of the same date, the President and aide John D. Ehrlichman discussed the statement Mr. Nixon would make.

"Four weeks ago, we—" the President began, and then said: "Why don't we say, shall we set a date? That sounds a hell of a lot stronger if we set a date."

"All right," Ehrlichman said.

"On March 21, I began new inquiries—strike that," the President said. "I ordered an investigation, new inquiries throughout the government—"

"How about saying," Ehrlichman suggested, "On March 21 as a result of serious charges which were reported publicly and—"

In subsequent statements, Mr. Nixon has said his own investigation was undertaken on March 21 as the date on which he first learned from John W. Dean III of White House involvement in the Watergate cover-up.

LATE RETURNS
May 18, 1973

"NATIONAL SECURITY"
May 22, 1973

May 23, 1973

**"LET'S LOOK AT THE BRIGHT SIDE
—MAYBE IT'S TAKING PEOPLE'S
MINDS OFF INFLATION"**

May 24, 1973

NATIONAL-SECURITY BLANKET

May 27, 1973

**"IT WAS ALL SO PATRIOTIC THAT
HE COULDN'T TRUST ANYONE BUT
HIS OWN BURGLARS"**

May 31, 1973

On April 30, Nixon went on television in a more determined effort to put "Watergate" in the past.

Beginning "I want to talk to you tonight from my heart," he told of how he had "personally ordered those conducting the investigations to get all the facts and to report them directly to me, right here in this office."

He also described a difficult decision: his acceptance of the resignations of "two of my closest associates in the White House—Bob Haldeman, John Ehrlichman—two of the finest public servants it has been my privilege to know." Less than a year later both were indicted by a federal grand jury. He went on to tell of the departure of Attorney General Kleindienst, "a distinguished public servant, my personal friend

"THERE MUST BE SOMETHING WRONG WITH THE CALCULATOR—THESE DON'T ADD UP EITHER"

May 30, 1973

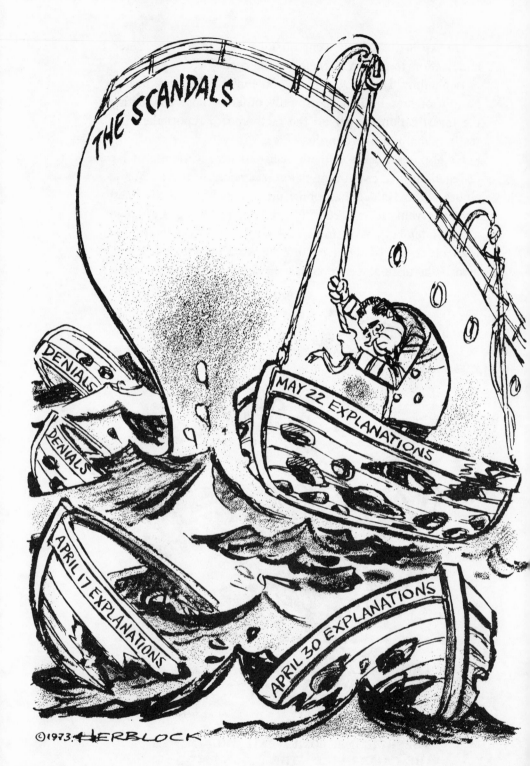

THE SCANDALS

DENIALS

DENIALS

MAY 22 EXPLANATIONS

APRIL 17 EXPLANATIONS

APRIL 30 EXPLANATIONS

©1973. HERBLOCK

May 25, 1973

"I AM AUTHORIZED TO SAY, 'WHAT WHALE?'"

June 5, 1973

"THEY NEEDED THEIR OWN SECRET POLICE TO WATCH THE SECRET OPERATIVES THEY HIRED TO ORGANIZE PHONY DEMONSTRATIONS AGAINST THEMSELVES . . ."

June 6, 1973

"DEAR—GUESS WHAT? TODAY THEY SAID THEY'D LET ME PERJURE MYSELF FOR THE LEADER!"

June 10, 1973

FLOOR-TO-CEILING CARPETING

June 12, 1973

"AND IF YOU GO TO SAN CLEMENTE, DON'T ASK IF THE PEOPLE PROVIDED HIM WITH THAT PROPERTY"

June 14, 1973

for 20 years, with no involvement whatever in this matter," and simply stated, "The Counsel to the President, John Dean, has also resigned."

The new Attorney General, he said, would be Elliot Richardson, and "I have given him absolute authority to make all decisions bearing upon the prosecution of the Watergate case and related matters."

Before concluding with a statement about wanting the 1,361 days left in his term to be the best days in America's history, he pointed out that "the Watergate affair . . . has claimed far too much of my time and my attention." He added, "I must now turn my full attention—once again—to the larger duties of this office."

"The larger duties" included a speech at a Republican fund-raising dinner nine days later. "Let me say," he told the audience, "I don't stand here tonight as a loser. We stand here tonight as winners."

This came from a "winner" who had felt it necessary to corrupt a national political system in scoring that win.

"WE ARE POOR LITTLE LAMBS WHO HAVE LOST OUR WAY. BLAH—BLAH—BLAH—"

June 15, 1973

"REMEMBER, MEN— THIS IS THE ONE THAT COUNTS"

June 21, 1973

June 24, 1973

June 26, 1973

At the time of Dean's testimony before the Senate Watergate Committee.

The efforts to "put Watergate behind us" were like those of a man who has stepped on a piece of flypaper, and is trying to kick it away.

The "Watergate affair" was getting stickier all the time, despite presidential statements and television appearances.

Soon the home screen would feature other people giving a different picture of what had been going on.

Nixon had reason to fear a congressional committee for what it might disclose—but even more for what it might broadcast. He applied full White House pressure to prevent an investigation by Wright Patman's House Banking and Currency Committee before the 1972 election. But what he wound up with may have been even worse for him: the Senate Watergate Committee under Chairman Sam Ervin (D-N.C.)—on television, live!

All those American living rooms which Mr. Nixon had entered via television, were now being entered, via the same medium, by men who broke into Watergate; by "President's men" who told about how they dug up dirt on political op-

"NOW WE ISSUE ANOTHER STATEMENT ABOUT HOW YOUR TRUSTED COUNSEL WAS TRYING TO COVER HIMSELF—RIGHT?"
June 28, 1973

June 29, 1973

**"IN RETROSPECT, LOOKING BACK,
AND WITH HINDSIGHT—"**

July 12, 1973

©1973 HERBLOCK

July 13, 197

**"WE'RE IN THE PROTECTION
BUSINESS. YOUR FOUR-YEAR-POLICY
WILL BE $100,000"**

July 8, 1973

Many corporate executives told of illegal contributions made as a result of solicitations by Nixon fund raisers. The board chairman of American Airlines said, "I was solicited by Mr. Herbert Kalmbach, who said that we were among those from whom $100,000 was expected. I knew Mr. Kalmbach to be . . . the President's personal counsel . . ."

ponents, carried around suitcases, briefcases, and little black bags of $100 bills, solicited dirty-tricksters, issued illegal orders from the White House, and covered up misdeeds. And they spoke thousands of words which were worth every bit as much as the pictures.

In their testimony, a picture unfolded of government leaders who cared nothing for the privacy of individual citizens, but who desperately needed privacy for their own activities. They acted as if the U.S. government was their private property—a sort of official-family business, something like the Corleones' in *The Godfather*.

Americans learned things Nixon had never mentioned in his many television appearances: about "wire men" (who planted taps and bugs); about an "enemies list"; and about burn bags and "deep-sixing" (means of getting rid of evidence). They learned about the stashing of bags of payoff money in phone booths, and about packets of $100 bills, numbered in sequence. (The $100 bill became so identified with Nixon campaign activities, that his picture seemed to belong

"I KNOW YOU'RE A NEWSMAN, BUT I FORGET IF THEY SMEARED YOU, PUT THE FBI ON YOU, TAPPED YOUR PHONE, OR AUDITED YOUR TAX RETURNS"
July 1, 1973

July 4, 1973

©1973 HERBLOCK

**"REMEMBER, NOT A WORD TO HIM ABOUT SORDID
POLITICAL ACTIVITIES"**

July 11, 1973

on it—and in a couple of cartoons I put it there).

Stories about Watergate and the White House now came flooding over the airwaves and pouring out of the television sets.

But with the exception of John Dean's testimony, there seemed to be a pervasive awe or fear of the President.

Throughout the Watergate hearings and subsequent trials and interviews, some White House aides and associates who had been engaged in crimes managed to come across as clean-cut young men who had somehow made a mistake. In most cases they seemed to show little understanding of what had been wrong. One of them regretted that he had served his President badly. The fact is that all of them served their country badly by serving that President too well.

A bigger fish in the Watergate net was former Attorney General John Mitchell, who stood by his old friend and chief, the President. We learned later that the President had early in the game decided he might solve his Watergate problems by making his old friend Mitchell a prime sacrifice.

"THEY MUST HAVE LAUNDERED OUR MONEY TOO— IT KEEPS SHRINKING"

July 15, 1973

"WE ARE OUTRAGED THAT A HOAX SHOULD HAVE BEEN PERPETRATED WITHOUT WHITE HOUSE AUTHORIZATION"

July 20, 1973

"YOU CAN SAY THAT AGAIN"
July 17, 1973

On the disclosure that Nixon had bugged his
own offices.

THE UNRAVELING
July 18, 1973

Referring to the Watergate crimes, Mitchell testified that "knowing Richard Nixon, the President, as I do, he would just lower the boom on all this matter and it would come back to hurt him and it would affect him in his re-election."

Sen. Herman Talmadge (D-Ga.) asked Mitchell if "the expediency of the election" was more important than telling Nixon that "all around him were people involved in crime, perjury, [and] accessory after the fact. . . ."

Mitchell responded: "Senator, I think you have put it exactly correct. . . ."

The Nixon-Mitchell relationship was apparently one of such mutual awe that neither dared to trouble the other. According to Mitchell, he did not discuss political matters with Nixon. And when questioned about his contacts with Mitchell, Nixon later explained that "The President doesn't pick up the phone and call the Attorney General every time something comes up on a matter." This indicated a distance of which Martha Mitchell was unaware, having frequently heard her husband wakened by presidential phone calls.

"OKAY, NOW CLOSE THIS ONE"

July 24, 1973

"WE NOW CAN TELL YOU THAT HE WAS SOFT ON THREATS TO NATIONAL SECURITY"

July 26, 1973

"HERE I AM, COPPER"

July 27, 1973

THE WHITE HOUSE
WASHINGTON

Operation Doctor's File
☑ Approved
"if ... it is not
traceable"

GOOD HOUSEBREAKING
SEAL OF APPROVAL

July 25, 1973

The picture Mitchell drew of a Nixon remote from political matters brought to mind the words of the late Oscar Levant when asked if he knew Doris Day. "Do I know Doris Day?" he exclaimed—"I knew her before she became a virgin."

A sensational disclosure of the hearings was the testimony of former deputy assistant to the President, Alexander Butterfield, who revealed that Nixon had the presidential offices bugged and tapped, so that everything said would be on tape. It was these tapes that eventually unraveled the Nixon presidency.

But at first, the tapes played a part in the massive White House campaign to discredit John Dean, whose detailed testimony was most damaging to Nixon.

Former Nixon aide H. R. (Bob) Haldeman told a flabbergasted committee (which had been denied tapes it requested for its investigation) that tapes had been loaned to him after he left the White House. He cited one of them to

"MOVE OVER—WE CAN'T STAY IN A HOLDING PATTERN FOREVER"
July 29, 1973

"NOT AT ALL—IT'S A PRIVILEGE"
July 31, 1973

COVER-UP III, PHASE II
August 1, 1973

SUNRISE AT SAN CLEMENTE
August 7, 1973

THE OVERLOADED SHREDDER
August 8, 1973

refute Dean's testimony that Nixon had discussed the raising of a million dollars in hush money.

Haldeman testified that Dean had neglected to mention that Nixon added, "We can do that, but it would be wrong."

Later, the tapes actually showed that in the conversation with Dean, Nixon had followed the talk about hush money with a discussion of the feasibility of clemency after the 1974 election. He had said, "It would be wrong, that's for sure." But he meant wrong only in the sense that a proposed clemency plan wouldn't work because of political backlash it would create. Nowhere did Nixon say that $1 million in cash for blackmail would be wrong.

This disclosure was one of those lightning flashes that illuminates an entire scene. In the lexicon of the Nixon White House, there was no "right" and "wrong" in the traditional sense of accepted morality or of what was good for the country. What was "right" was whatever would work; what was "wrong" was whatever would result in getting caught. That explanation of a single phrase told the story of five and a half years of national leadership.

**"GOOD MORNING, FOLKS—
—NOW FOR THE LATEST NEWS—"**

August 9, 1973

**"NOW, IS EVERYTHING
PERFECTLY CLEAR?"**

August 16, 1973

DELAYED-ACTION BOMB

August 12, 1973

"HOW MANY 'GREAT DAYS FOR AMERICA' ARE LEFT ON THAT SECOND-TERM CALENDAR THE CHIEF GAVE US?"

August 14, 1973

"I have been informed that I am under investigation for possible violations of the criminal statutes. I will make no further comment until the investigation has been completed, other than to say that I am innocent of any wrongdoing, that I have confidence in the criminal justice system of the United States and I am equally confident that my innocence will be affirmed."
—Vice President Spiro Agnew, August 6.

The most damaging witness against Nixon was Nixon himself.

Even before the tapes and transcripts, readings of Nixon addresses, statements, and press conference remarks revealed many discrepancies. They were too many, in fact, for anyone to keep up with.

On August 15, 1973, in his public statements on hush money, Nixon said he had been told that money was being paid to defendants only for legal support, not to procure silence.

But half a year later he said he *was* told that hush money had been paid.

Shortly afterward, he said he didn't have *knowledge* that money was paid—only Dean's *allegation* that it was paid. This revision apparently had to do with the legal consequences implicit in "knowledge" of a crime.

Finally, we learned—via tapes and expurgated transcripts—that in speaking of hush money needed for E. Howard Hunt, Nixon ordered Dean, "Well for Christ's sakes get it in a,

"I HEREBY GRANT YOU EXECUTIVE CLEMENCY"

August 17, 1973

"HE WANTS US TO FORGET WATERGATE AND GET BACK TO FORGETTING HIS ECONOMIC GAME PLANS, FALSE BOMBING REPORTS, WHEAT DEAL, SAN CLEMENTE . . ."

August 19, 1973

THE MAKING OF A PRESIDENTIAL CAMPAIGN

August 2, 1973

in a way that, uh—Who's, who's going to talk to him? Colson? He's the one who's supposed to know him."

While trying to put Watergate behind him, Nixon decided he had to put behind him his Vice President, who was involved in scandals of his own. These began in Maryland, where Agnew had held office, and extended to receiving money handed to him over the vice presidential desk. When one "contributor" who was involved in contracts complained to the Vice President that an Agnew associate was also pressing him for a $10,000 contribution, Agnew replied, "Say you gave at the office."

When Agnew left that office, I had no more desire to draw cartoons celebrating the event than I did when Nixon was defeated in 1960 or in 1962. I was glad that he was

"OF COURSE, THAT DOESN'T INCLUDE TURNING OVER THE EVIDENCE"
August 21, 1973

GENERAL SERVICES ADMINISTRATION

SAN CLEMENTE IMPROVEMENTS

STATE DEPT.

WITHHOLDING OF CANADIAN GOVT. INFORMATION ON PIPELINE

U.S. TREASURY

TAX WRITE-OFF FOR NIXON "PAPERS"

POLITICIZING OF THE U.S. SECRET SERVICE

PENTAGON

14 MONTHS OF FALSIFIED REPORTS ON BOMBINGS OF CAMBODIA

THE NIXON SCANDALS

©1973 HERBLOCK

WIDENING FLOOD AREA

August 3, 1973

If it were not for the corruption and corrosion of so many other institutions, I'd have given more space to the fall of the Secret Service. Formerly one of the most highly respected organizations in the country, this outfit became completely politicized—eager to please the leader in any way. The Secret Service operated taping machines and it harassed political dissenters. It put its anti-counterfeiting function to political use by attempting to stop the manufacture or publication of items satirizing the President, if they had even a vague resemblance to currency. In one case they confiscated large quantities of coffee mugs bearing a caricature of Nixon on a design of a "three-dollar bill" imprinted on the mug itself. The Secret Service has not only become ripe for congressional investigation, but over-ripe.

out. And it seemed more important to remind people that getting rid of Agnew and others close to the President did not exculpate Nixon, who was responsible for putting them in positions of power.

Agnew resigned in a deal by which he was allowed to plead *nolo contendere* to a charge of income tax evasion, on condition that the prosecution would release a forty-page statement of evidence for which he might have been prosecuted.

Following the Agnew resignation, Nixon nominated House Minority leader Gerald R. Ford to be Vice President.

Almost any selection of a new Vice President by Nixon at that time would have troubled me.

Nixon was involved in so many scandals, and his own unfitness for high office was so clear that it did not seem to me

"THANK GOD THERE'S BEEN NO PERSONAL GAIN INVOLVED . . ."

August 23, 1973

While he was presiding at the trial of Daniel Ellsberg, Judge Matthew Byrne was twice invited to San Clemente, where he was offered the directorship of the FBI.

ABOVE ANY OFFICE
August 31, 1973

**"AS I'VE ALWAYS SAID: 'WE MUST GET
THE STORY OUT, THE TRUTH OUT'"**
August 24, 1973

he should choose a possible successor.

The 25th Amendment, under which he made the nomination, was not ratified until 1967, and could hardly have come into play under worse circumstances: a corrupt President naming someone to replace his corrupt Vice President.

As for Ford himself, he was a genial man but strongly partisan. When Nixon nominee G. Harrold Carswell was rejected for the Supreme Court, Ford immediately began an all-out effort to have Justice William O. Douglas impeached. Later, when impeachment of Nixon was being considered, Ford insisted to the very end that there were no grounds for such action.

The 25th amendment does not require the Congress to ratify any presidential selection. But Democrats feared that they might be accused of partisanship if their own Speaker of the

TAPE JOB
August 28, 1973

"EXECUTIVEPRIVILEGE, SEPARATIONOFPOWERS,
NATIONALSECURITY, CONFIDENTIALITY,
ABRACADABRA— DISAPPEAR!"

September 13, 1973

House remained next in line of succession while Congress and the President hashed over a vice presidential choice.

Congress was reluctant to show any muscle even in so important a matter as the selection of a possible successor to Nixon. And Ford was genuinely popular with his fellow congressmen.

Another factor in the congressional desire to fill the vice presidential vacancy was an event that occurred less than two weeks after Agnew's resignation and Ford's nomination.

This was the "Saturday Night Massacre."

When Nixon ordered that Special Prosecutor Archibald Cox be fired, Attorney General Elliot Richardson refused to do it and resigned. Deputy Attorney General William Ruckelshaus also refused and also left. Solicitor General Robert Bork then became acting Attorney General and carried out Nixon's order.

BIG BROTHER
September 7, 1973

"IF IT HAS SOMETHING TO DO WITH THE FUEL SHORTAGE, WHY AREN'T THE REST OF THE EXECUTIVE OFFICES LIKE THIS?"
September 19, 1973

'AND STOP SAYING, 'WHAT ELSE CAN HAPPEN?' "

September 23, 1973

"I DIDN'T REALIZE THE HEARINGS WERE ON AGAIN"

September 25, 1973

September 27, 1973

"HELLO, ANGELA DAVIS? YOU MAY BE A LITTLE SURPRISED TO HEAR FROM ME . . ."

October 2, 1973

In the wake of the Cox firing, the move for impeachment began picking up steam. And in the face of this "firestorm," Nixon suddenly decided to obey a court order that he give up some evidence to Judge Sirica.

But two of the nine tapes promised to the Judge were then declared by the White House to be nonexistent. A week later it developed that despite all the White House talk about secrecy and confidentiality, the tapes had—according to White House accounts—been loaned out or passed around with records of their whereabouts consisting of occasional jottings on scraps of paper resembling parts of old brown bags.

Less than three weeks after *that,* the nation learned that on one of the other tapes there was an eighteen-and-a-half-minute erasure of a crucial Watergate conversation.

Nixon was now entangled in his own tapes. And with the inauguration of his new Vice President, the reel of his own time in the White House had eight months left to run. ■

"OH, THE THINGS YOU SEE SPREAD AROUND—INNUENDOS, ACCUSATIONS, ATTACKS!"
October 4, 1973

"HE'S A SPLENDID PRESIDENT—I WAS ONLY COMPLAINING ABOUT THOSE UNSCRUPULOUS CRUMMY NIXON ADMINISTRATION PEOPLE HE EMPLOYS"
October 7, 1973

THE SIDE-SHOW CLOSES
October 11, 1973

On Agnew's forced resignation.

©1973 HERBLOCK

"AND IF YOU SHOULD BECOME PRESIDENT, WILL YOU
FAITHFULLY PROTECT AND DEFEND THE RECORDS,
FILES, TAX RETURNS, AND TAPES OF THE PRESIDENT
WHO NAMED YOU?"

October 12, 1973

"YOU WOULDN'T HAVE ANY QUESTION ABOUT A SELECTION OF MINE, WOULD YOU?"

October 14, 1973

"YES, GERALD FORD, YOU ALSO WIN THIS OFFICIAL SEAL, THIS
BOX OF TV MAKEUP, THIS LIMOUSINE, WITH CHAUFFEUR—
AND WAIT, THAT'S NOT ALL—A COMPLETE SET OF SECRET SERVICE
MEN, PLUS THREE YEARS, EXPENSES PAID, IN THE
SECOND HIGHEST OFFICE IN THE LAND—"

October 16, 1973

©1973 HERBLOCK

October 17, 1973

Agnew's immobile face and the way he bared his lower teeth prompted me, while watching him on television one evening, to doodle sketches of him as a shark, but I had never tried to bend the cartoons to include this caricature.

On Agnew's departure from office, when even this shark was small-fry compared to the greater predator still at large, I finally found occasion to use the caricature I had doodled long before.

"YOU GOT ALL THE BAGS, BEBE?"
October 19, 1973

NOW, IS EVERYTHING PERFECTLY . . ."
September 2, 1973

MORAL TONE
August 30, 1973

©1973 HERBLOCK

MUGGING
October 23, 1973

On the "Saturday Night Massacre."

**"LOOK—NICE TAPES—OKAY,
BOY?—OKAY?—"**
October 24, 1973

**"CHIEF—THE BACKSWING
—LOOK OUT—"**

October 25, 1973

**"FOLLOWING THIS NEWEST
GOVERNMENT CRISIS, WE
NOW RESUME WITH THE LATEST
ADMINISTRATION SCANDALS"**

October 26, 1973

"I HAVE WHAT IT TAKES"

October 30, 1973

**"NOW WE'll PUT IN A NEW
LAWMAN THAT WE CAN
COOPERATE WITH"**

October 28, 1973

October 31, 1973

**"NOW, IF YOU JUST PUT
THIS ON AND LISTEN
VERY CAREFULLY—"**
November 2, 1973

"POOF!"
November 1, 1973

November 5, 1973

"ONLY A TOUGH GUY LIKE ME
CAN HANDLE THIS CASE—YOU
KNOW HOW PERMISSIVE
THE COURTS ARE"
November 6, 1973

"YES, CHIEF—EVEN WITH
THE FUEL SHORTAGE THE
PEOPLE SEEM TO
BE PLENTY WARM"
November 11, 1973

"THEY WERE SO CONFIDENTIAL
THAT WE DIDN'T WRITE
DOWN WHO WE PASSED
THEM AROUND TO"
November 7, 1973

"IF YOU HADN'T BEEN SO BUSY
WITH TAPS AND TAPES, YOU
MIGHT HAVE HEARD
THEM COMING"
November 9, 1973

**"UH—YOU'RE NEW HERE.
WE HAVEN'T BEEN REFERRING
TO IT QUITE THAT WAY"**

September 30, 1973

"THAT'S INFLATIONARY"

September 21, 1973

BACKGROUND NOISES

November 13, 1973

**"NOW, THIS TIME, TO
CLEAR UP EVERYTHING—"**

November 14, 1973

FULL DISCLOSURE
November 18, 1973

**"WE ALL HAVE OUR
BURDENS TO BEAR"**
November 21, 1973

"FORWARD!"
November 23, 1973

"AS I WAS SAYING, IT'S TERRIBLE THE WAY PRESIDENTIAL CANDIDATES AND POLITICAL CONVENTIONS PICK VICE PRESIDENTS"

November 22, 1973

Nixon's selection of Ford was approved by the Senate 92–3; and by the House 387–35.

"—AND THEN, AFTER THAT—"
November 25, 1973

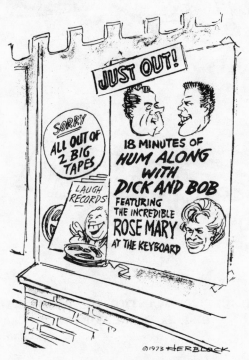

RECORD SHOP
November 28, 1973

"ARE YOU SURE YOU WANT TO WEAR THIS INTO YOUR
RE-ELECTION CAMPAIGN?"

December 2, 1973

FIRM HAND AT THE HELM
November 27, 1973

**"SHE TRIED PUSHING A TAPE
RECORDER BUTTON WHILE
HOLDING HER FOOT ON A PEDAL
AND REACHING BACK FOR A
TELEPHONE—"**
November 30, 1973

**"WELL, BOSS, NOBODY CAN SAY
YOU'RE INCAPABLE OF LEADING"**
December 5, 1973

**"NOW, ONCE MORE—
WATCH CLOSELY—"**
December 6, 1973

**"YOU'RE DOING FINE—
EVENTUALLY IT'S BOUND
TO GET TIRED."**

August 15, 1973

**"OH—UH—I'M SANTA CLAUS, HO
HO HO—COME TO LEAVE YOU A
MENTION IN MY WILL"**

December 11, 1973

**"THAT'S WHERE WE MISSED OUT—
WE DIDN'T PICK OUR OWN
JUDGES AND JURIES"**

December 13, 1973

"VERY INTERESTING"

December 16, 1973

SHORTAGE
December 18, 1973

"YOU MIGHT AS WELL TAKE A WRITE-OFF ON THE WHOLE THING—IT'S BEEN DEPRECIATING SINCE 1969"
December 27, 1973

"HE'S GOT ME WORRIED ABOUT ANOTHER KIND OF CAPITAL GAINS AND LOSSES"
December 23, 1973

"YOU KNOW WHAT? I'M TIRED OF HIM AND ALL HIS CRISES"
December 28, 1973

THE NON-SHORTAGE

January 3, 1974

**"WELL, THAT WAS A SHORT RUN.
WHAT'S NEXT?"**

January 6, 1974

THE TAPE
PLAYS OUT

During Nixon's time as President, one law caught up with him—the law of diminishing returns. The television appearances and the explanations continued, but credibility kept diminishing.

1974

Nevertheless, he continued his old policy of "attack, attack, attack" which had served in so many campaigns.

As the scandals developed, Nixon & Co. accused the press of "character assassination," of being irresponsible, and of basing stories on "rumor, gossip and innuendo." Nixon referred to the "leers and sneers" of commentators—"which is their perfect right." Television news contained the most "outrageous, vicious, distorted reporting" he had heard in twenty-seven years of public life, but "I'm not blaming anyone for that." Congressional committees were accused of being prejudiced and putting out damaging leaks. Later, Patrick Buchanan, special consultant to the President, claimed that the federal grand jury in Washington, D.C., was unfair, because Washington was an "anti-Nixon city," and many mem-

©1974 HERBLOCK

END OF ANOTHER REEL
January 16, 1974

©1974 HERBLOCK

RUBBED OUT
January 17, 1974

bers of the grand jury were black.

January began with the scrapping of what was popularly known as "Operation Candor"—a policy of slightly less concealment.

A panel of electronic experts which had investigated the famous "18½-minute hum" reported its findings. The experts found that there had been five or more separate erasures and re-recordings on that section of tape.

The White House—and some newspaper writers—referred to these electronic specialists as "the court experts" and even "Sirica's experts." But the six-man panel had been agreed upon by representatives of Nixon and Special Prosecutor Leon Jaworski. When Nixon counsel James St. Clair declared that the White House would get its own experts, one of the panel replied, "We thought *we* were your experts."

In his State of the Union message later that month, Nixon said: "One year of Watergate is enough." But it would not go away.

On March 1, seven former Nixon aides were indicted by a federal grand jury. These included Haldeman, Ehrlichman, and Mitchell—all for conspiracy, perjury, and obstruction

"ERASE THOSE THOUGHTS"
January 18, 1974

"IF YOU LISTEN VERY CLOSELY, YOU CAN HEAR A VOICE SAYING, 'I AM NOT A CROOK, I AM NOT A CROOK, I AM . . .'"
January 20, 1974

**"CHIEF, WE'RE PICKING UP SOME
NICE COMMENTS ABOUT
YOUR STATEMENT IN FAVOR OF
INDIVIDUAL PRIVACY"**

February 5, 1974

**GOT TO CLOSE OFF ROOMS, TURN
OFF LIGHTS—THE ENERGY
SHORTAGE, YOU KNOW"**

January 13, 1974

WHITE HOUSE SECRET EVIDENCE

January 27, 1974

Sen. Scott said he had seen "information" the
White House possessed, which would exculpate
Nixon completely on "specific items."

**"THE ALLEGATIONS ARE
UTTERLY FALSE—
I'VE ONLY BEEN
INVOLVED UP TO HERE"**

January 10, 1974

of justice. Others indicted were former White House special counsel Charles W. Colson, former White House aide Gordon Strachan, former "CREEP" attorney Kenneth W. Parkinson, and former Assistant Attorney General Robert C. Mardian.

April was income-tax month, and for Nixon a particularly bad one because his back taxes caught up with him. Nothing had struck so close to home with so many Americans as the discovery that he had contrived to pay almost no income taxes, although the presidential salary alone came to $200,000 a year, plus $50,000 a year for his own expenses—plus a nontaxable $40,000 for official travel and entertainment. The Internal Revenue Service had originally approved Nixon's 1970 and 1971 returns and praised him on having them so well prepared. The IRS agent who wrote the letter of praise received a promotion.

In the previous year, newspaper accounts had reported enough about Nixon's finances that he felt obliged to disclose some of his tax returns. Once more he selected his own jury—the Joint Congressional Committee on Internal Revenue and Taxation—to determine if he owed anything.

The IRS also went over his returns again.

"I KEEP HEARING AN ECHO OR SOMETHING"
January 23, 1974

"WHY, THEY ASKED FOR SOME TAPES THAT DON'T EVEN HAVE A HUM IN THEM YET"
February 6, 1974

"HAIL TO THE CHIEF"
January 25, 1974

Both the congressional committee and the IRS reported, in April 1974, that he owed more than $450,000 in back taxes and interest.

One of the major deductions disallowed was for the contribution of some of his vice presidential papers to the government. These had been turned over under highly unusual circumstances—and also involved the back-dating of a deed after the tax laws made such a gift nondeductible.

Nixon's tax lawyer, Frank DeMarco, Jr. (a partner of Nixon lawyer Herbert Kalmbach) later testified that Nixon —a former tax lawyer himself—had gone over his returns, line by line. Nixon had said at the Associated Press Managing Editors Association meeting a few months before that he didn't take "deductions for, shall we say, a cattle ranch or interest or all of these gimmicks . . ."

But he *had* taken deductions for interest—and gimmicks —and everything else allowable—and a great deal that was not allowable.

However, the IRS made no finding of fraud.

The congressional committee selected by Nixon to go over his returns, headed by Rep. Wilbur Mills (D-Ark.) and Sen. Russell Long (D-La.), said it had no business deciding on fraud.

"DEAR, DID YOU KNOW THAT $290,000 OF OUR TAX MONEY HAS ALREADY BEEN SPENT ON HIS LEGAL DEFENSE TEAM?"
February 12, 1974

"WHAT KIND OF MERRY-GO-ROUND IS THIS?"
February 15, 1974

STATE OF THE UNION

January 30, 1974

In answering a question about his finances, at a Nov. 24, 1973 press conference with managing editors at Disney World, Nixon said, "I welcome this kind of examination, because the people have got to know whether or not their President is a crook. Well, I am not a crook."

Ultimately the House Judiciary Committee would vote down an article of impeachment based on Nixon's personal finances because—as his defenders explained—the IRS and the congressional committee hadn't found fraud.

As one committee member said, the buck stopped nowhere.

While the sentiment for impeachment rose, Nixon continued to appear on television from time to time, not only to give his versions of personal and political affairs but to offer his own special versions of history as well.

In one statement, he referred to what he called the "Jefferson precedent" of not making evidence available to a court. Historians, and even historical societies, pointed out that Jefferson, far from defying the court, had simply declined to make the trip to deliver in person a letter which he had been called on to produce. But he provided the letter, complete and unedited. In a subsequent broadcast, Nixon—aware that more people heard him on television than read history books—blandly made the same statement again, this time calling it "the Jefferson *rule*."

Nixon said: "Every President since George Washington has tried to protect the confidentiality of Presidential con-

February 1, 1974

**"DON'T WORRY—I'M
GOING TO HANG ON"**
February 20, 1974

**"YOU UNDERSTAND HOW
IT IS, MOM"**

February 27, 1974

OBSTACLE COURSE

February 19, 1974

versations and you remember the famous case involving Thomas Jefferson . . ." Nixon implied that his "rule" applied even to House Judiciary Committee subpoenas—even though all of our previous Presidents had indicated nothing could be withheld from an impeachment inquiry.

Such instant historical revision, going back to the first President, suggested all kinds of possibilities—like a rewrite of the cherry-tree story in which little George might say to his father, "I can not tell a lie; I will say candidly and clearly that this orchard is infested with beavers."

To the injuries he inflicted on the Judiciary Committee, Nixon now added insult.

On April 29, he appeared on all major network screens accompanied by a set piece: an arrangement of dozens of gold-embossed binders containing edited transcripts of some of the tapes which had been subpoenaed. He sounded as if he were performing an act of unprecedented generosity in offering these partial transcriptions of *sections* of *some* of the subpoenaed tapes instead of the evidence called for. As he spoke, the camera kept panning back to the stacks of "transcripts" as if we were being urged to buy a volume with every bag of groceries. We did not learn until the next

"I THINK I'LL WRITE A BOOK ABOUT MY SIX PROBLEMS"
February 28, 1974

AT THE HELM
March 1, 1974

©1974 HERBLOCK

March 3, 1974

On the March 1 indictment of seven former Nixon aides, including Haldeman, Ehrlichman, and Mitchell.

day that what all those impressive binders contained were what the Government Printing Office was putting out as one paperback volume, and what the *Chicago Tribune* was able to print the next day in a single forty-four-page section of that newspaper.

Overnight a few parenthetical words became household words: (inaudible), (unintelligible), and (expletive deleted). There were also words like "stonewalling," and strange phrases like "taking the hangout road" (for telling the truth, or letting it all hang out), and then "limited modified hangouts"—for, well, cover-ups.

A realization grew that if the impeachment committee ever got its hands on the actual tapes it requested, we might have our first X-rated President.

St. Clair gave the press a "summary" of the transcripts, which, he said, cleared Nixon. It was probably assumed that few people would actually read much of the transcripts. Many did, and they found that what St. Clair had told the public was misleading.

When St. Clair first went on the public payroll, he said he was defending "the presidency"—then, later, decided his client was "the President." Lawyer St. Clair served as lobbyist and

**"YES, SIR, CHIEF—
THAT'S GOOD NEWS"**
March 7, 1974

STREAKING
March 6, 1974

March 12, 1974

**"THERE IT IS, JUST THE WAY IT
CAME OFF THE FOUNDING
FATHERS' TYPEWRITER"**

March 13, 1974

propagandist. And his statements to the Supreme Court and to the House Judiciary Committee that they had been given all the relevant evidence were inaccurate.

As a long succession of Nixon aides and campaign workers were indicted or convicted or pleaded guilty, and as the evidence against Nixon mounted, his defenders cried that he was being "prejudged." They said he was being accused of "guilt by association"—that is, by association with those who did his bidding.

This was a far cry from the "guilt by association" of the early 1950s, when Nixon had helped whip up hysteria and suspicion of Communist taint in connection with people guilty of nothing.

Nixon defenders claimed he was the victim of wrongdoing by eager aides whose "zeal exceeded their judgment,"

**"I WILL CONTINUE TO COOPERATE
COMPLETELY IN PROVIDING ANY
UNSHREDDED, UNLOST AND UNERASED
EVIDENCE I AM ABSOLUTELY FORCED TO
GIVE UP"**

March 8, 1974

"AS FAR AS THE IRS IS CONCERNED, THE PRESIDENT IS JUST ANOTHER CITIZEN."
—Richard M. Citizen

"HO HUM—JUST ANOTHER CITIZEN TAKING A WRITE-OFF ON $576,000 IN ASSORTED PAPERS, WITH A LITTLE BACK-DATING ON THE DEED"

March 19, 1974

YOU WILL BE BETTER ADVISED TO WATCH WHAT WE DO THAN WHAT WE SAY
— Atty. Gen. Mitchell 1969

IT'S NOT WHAT WE SAY OR DO, BUT WHAT WE SAY WE KNOW WE MEANT

March 15, 1974

ON THE AIR

APPLAUSE

NIXON FREE-TV ROAD SHOW

THE HUSH MONEY

"SHHHH!"

March 17, 1974

as he had put it. Cases of unbelievable innocence are commonly summed up in the example of the fellow who had played a piano in a bawdy house for years without knowing what was going on upstairs. In Nixon's case we were, in effect, told that he not only had played that piano for five years, but that he had rented the house, hired the girls, sent out the men to solicit, and greeted guests in the parlor without knowing what was going on in that house.

Gov. Nelson Rockefeller, who never found anything to alarm him in what was going on, got big hands from partisan audiences by declaring that in our country every man is presumed innocent until proven guilty—even if he happens to be President of the United States.

This sounded fine. And nobody wanted to do injustice to a poor old President of the United States, who only had under him the Justice Department, the FBI, the CIA, as-

"IMAGINE THAT CONGRESSIONAL COMMITTEE WANTING TO GET 42 TAPES OUT OF THE WHITE HOUSE"
March 27, 1974

In press conferences, Nixon spoke of the House Judiciary Committee wanting to bring a "U-Haul trailer" to the White House to haul out material.

"TO START WITH, WHY IS OUR TAX MONEY PAYING FOR HIS MOUTHPIECE?"

March 21, 1974

"WE'VE HAD SO MUCH EXPERIENCE INVESTIGATING OURSELVES, WE WANT TO HELP WITH YOUR INVESTIGATION TOO"

March 22, 1974

March 24, 1974

"ALL WE WANT TO DO IS CHECK THE IMPEACHMENT MACHINERY TO MAKE SURE IT'S WORKING RIGHT"

April 3, 1974

sorted press offices, millions of dollars worth of legal talent, and all the executive departments.

But what people like Gov. Rockefeller neglected to mention was that in our country no man is presumed to be above the law—even if he happens to be President.

Other Americans can not, without danger of penalty, refuse to appear before a grand jury, as Mr. Nixon did.

Other Americans *can* be indicted.

Other Americans can not set their own ground rules; and other Americans can not tell prosecutors, grand juries, congressional committees: We'll decide what evidence you need.

Other Americans can not fire special prosecutors.

So when people said Nixon must be presumed innocent, there was a kind of "Catch 22" gimmick there. They meant that he was innocent until proven guilty, but he couldn't be proven guilty as long as he was President.

**"YOU SEE THAT NEXT
SUMMIT YET, HENRY?"**
March 29, 1974

**"AND NOW, THE ENVELOPES,
PLEASE—PLEASE, THE
ENVELOPES—UNSHREDDED—"**

April 2, 1974

April 4, 1974

On the news that Nixon owed $467,000 in back
taxes and interest for the years 1969 through
1972.

Gov. Rockefeller's words about "proven guilty" suddenly became inoperative when Nixon became once more a private citizen, subject to full legal procedures. This public figure who would not call for a Nixon resignation because he believed everything should be done by "constitutional procedures" declared—almost immediately after being nominated for the vice presidency himself—that he believed it was enough that Nixon had given up his office.

The final mind-blowing twist to all this was later provided by President Ford. He said that, as he saw it, "a former President of the United States, instead of enjoying equal treatment with any other citizen accused of violating the law, would be cruelly and excessively penalized" in preserving the presumption of innocence.

In other words, Ford was telling us that in our country an EX-President couldn't get justice either.

In this political shell game there was never a good time to speak up about subversion of government, never a good time for the law to take its course, never a good time to let the public find out what Nixon's misdeeds included.

During the final year of his administration, the Multiple-

"AND SO, REMEMBER THE LESSON: HONESTY IS THE BEST POLICY IF NOTHING ELSE WORKS"
April 5, 1974

"A LITTLE BACKDATING ON A DEED—A FEW HUNDRED THOUSAND DOLLARS UNDERPAYMENT—WE ALL MAKE INNOCENT MISTAKES"
April 7, 1974

POSITION OF MORAL LEADERSHIP
April 13, 1974

Bad-Things-Advantage that Nixon had working for him now provided still another benefit. The misdeeds were so profuse and the disclosures so frequent that people became numbed by them.

As more and more outrages came to light, many became accustomed to a sensation-a-week diet, not of hyped-up journalism but of news that was really sensational.

A frequent frustrating experience during this period was being asked by someone, a few days after the shock of the latest exposure, "But do you think something will happen that will actually be an impeachable offense—something that will really *do* it?"

This was finally translated into congressional and journalistic demands for a "smoking gun"—meaning a crime as obvious, and witnessed by as many people, as the shooting of Lee Harvey Oswald by Jack Ruby.

There were enough misdeeds and sufficient evidence to make the Oval Office and the impeachment inquiry chambers "gunsmoke-filled" rooms. But for those who didn't want to see, it might not have been enough even if the gunsmoke had spelled out in skywriting, "I did it.—R.M.N."

Nixon had claimed "national security" as the reason for

"HERE'S TWO MORE RETURNS CLAIMING NIXON'S LAWYERS AS DEPENDENTS—AND HERE'S ONE SAYING, 'IF YOU FIND WHERE I'VE CHISELED, I'LL PAY'"

April 9, 1974

"HE'S RIGHT—WE SHOULD FORGET THE SCANDALS AND LET HIM GET ON WITH HIS ECONOMIC DISASTERS"

April 21, 1974

April 11, 1974

**THE MILLS OF THE GODS
GRIND SLOWLY......**

April 26, 1974

forming the "plumbers" unit, although illegal activities such as the break-in at Dr. Fielding's office had nothing to do with national security. But in the absence of testimony that Nixon had directed the actual participants, his defenders found him blameless.

What was wanted was a letter in which Nixon described where to order a crowbar and other tools and told specifically how, where, and at what time of night they were to be used. Instead, the boss had merely told the right people he wanted certain things done and didn't care how they were done.

And so it went—right through the impeachment committee hearings themselves.

It was in those hearings that William L. Hungate (D-Mo.) later said: "If a guy brought an elephant through that door and one of us said that is an elephant, some of the doubters would say, you know, that is an inference. That could be a mouse with a glandular condition."

April 18, 1974

On the loss of a Republican congressional race in Michigan, where Nixon had appeared personally in an effort to win the seat, or to take credit if it was won by a Republican. This marked the fifth loss of a Republican seat in 1974 special elections to Congress.

**"WHAT WOULD MAKE
ANYONE THINK I HAVE
ANYTHING TO CONCEAL?"**

April 28, 1974

INTERNAL JOB

April 29, 1974

In May, the House Judiciary Committee served notice that Nixon's defiance of its subpoenas for evidence might constitute grounds for impeachment. And in June it was disclosed that the federal grand jury which had indicted top Nixon aides had also named the President as an "unindicted co-conspirator."

Presidential trips to the Middle East and to Russia in June and July seemed more like flights from the home crisis than journeys for peace. As events at home went more and more badly, Nixon leaned more heavily than ever on his record abroad. But even this record was not as lustrous as it had seemed during his 1972 televised visits with heads of state.

Americans who believed their government had been scrupulous in observing Cambodian neutrality until the 1970 "incursion" had since learned of falsified reports that kept a

©1974 HERBLOCK

April 30, 1974

May 1, 1974

**"LISTEN, ARE YOU GOING TO
BE LOYAL TO ME OR
THAT (EXPLETIVE
DELETED) CONSTITUTION?"**

May 3, 1974

**"HERE'S THE SCENARIO. YOU GO
IN THERE, BLOW YOURSELF UP,
AND SPLIT THE WHOLE
PLACE DOWN THE MIDDLE"**

May 5, 1974

May 2, 1974

year of bombings of Cambodia secret—from Americans.

Indochina was not enjoying a "generation of peace," and the U.S. was not free of involvement there. "Peace with honor" had meant the withdrawal of American troops after four Nixon years in office and 20,000 more American dead. It also meant White House receptions for POWs—mostly career officer fliers—while returning GIs who had never been taken prisoner tried to find jobs or adequate medical care. Ending U.S. troop involvement—after four more years—was better than continuing it indefinitely. But one of the first voices that had been raised for introducing American troops into Indochina had been that of Vice President Nixon in 1954. And no major political figure had for so long done so much to promote the idea that a rapprochement with Russia or China would be the equivalent of a sellout.

Under the circumstances, it was a little as if the leader of a gang kept tossing bombs through the windows of a business firm until he was taken in as chairman of the board—and then praised for being the only person who could have ended intimidation by racketeers.

The Nixon administration's warm support for the Greek military junta, like its support for the Pakistani dictatorship,

"WOW—AND THIS IS WITH THE COVER ON"

May 8, 1974

"BOSS, IT'S NOT FLYING"

May 9, 1974

SHREDDING MACHINE
May 7, 1974

"HOLD THAT GANGPLANK!"
May 10, 1974

"THERE'S BEEN A LOT OF SILL*
TALK THAT OUR POSITION
IS ERODING"
May 12, 197

was a failure.

In late June, there was a Middle East trip highlighted by the turnout of millions of Egyptians. This was followed by another journey to Russia in July; and then the foreign tours of President Nixon came to an end.

Shortly after his return from Russia, he was faced with the fact that the House Judiciary Committee had found— even on those tapes in its possession—significant sections not included in his transcripts released April 29.

One section which had been omitted included Nixon's words of March 22, 1973: "I want you all to stonewall it, let them plead the Fifth Amendment, cover up or anything else, if it'll save it—save the plan." Of this deleted section, counsel St. Clair blandly said that it was "not that relevant." Press Secretary Ziegler echoed this theme by saying it was of "dubious relevance."

"OKAY, YOU GO OUT AND SPEAK FOR ME NEXT, THEN THE MAID —WHERE'S KING TIMAHOE?"

May 14, 1974

Publicly defending Nixon were his daughters, one of whom held a press conference, and a previously little known "White House priest" who had taken leave of clerical duties to serve as a Nixon propagandist.

**"WE DEPLORE THE VICIOUS
REPORTS ABOUT THE
PRESIDENTIAL REMARKS WE
REFUSE TO DISCLOSE"**

May 15, 1974

**"WE WANT EVERYTHING PUBLIC
EXCEPT THE EVIDENCE"**

May 17, 1974

**"IT'S LOOKING MORE AND MORE
LIKE A BIRD OF PREY"**

May 19, 1974

The technique now was not merely to cover up, but to pretend that what couldn't be covered up didn't amount to anything or wasn't actually there.

It was reminiscent of the scene in the movie *A Guide for the Married Man* in which Robert Morse explains to Walter Matthau the techniques for deceiving one's wife. In the "admit nothing" illustration, a shocked wife finds her husband in bed with another woman. Calmly and silently the husband and his companion dress and make up the bed, and his companion leaves. The husband then dons smoking jacket, lights his pipe, and peruses the newspaper. When his wife finds voice to ask, "What about that woman?" he raises his eyebrows and asks, "What woman?"

On July 25 came an event that led to the end of the Nixon administration. The Supreme Court ruled, 8-0, that Nixon must surrender tapes that had been subpoenaed by the Special Prosecutor.

On August 5, Nixon released new transcripts which revealed that shortly after the Watergate break-in, he had im-

"OF COURSE, THIS LOOKS BAD; BUT IT CAN'T HURT US AS MUCH AS GIVING THEM THE EVIDENCE"

May 23, 1974

May 31, 1974

May 24, 1974

**"DOES IT SEEM TO YOU TO BE
GETTING A LITTLE
CLOSE IN HERE?"**

June 4, 1974

peded an FBI investigation and had ordered his aides to cover up evidence that crimes had been committed.

That disclosure marked the collapse of his defense in Congress. Only a couple of the 435 members of the House of Representatives were reported to be still publicly opposed to impeachment; and Nixon was informed by his own party leaders that he probably could not muster more than 15 out of 100 votes in the Senate.

On August 8, he went on television to announce his resignation effective as of noon the next day, because, he said, "I no longer have a strong enough political base in Congress" to justify continuing the term in office "to which you elected me."

Most of the speech was about foreign policy and his

"YOUR WORK SEEMS TO BE CUT OUT FOR YOU"
May 28, 1974

©1974 HERBLOCK

May 26, 1974

efforts for peace, with one other elliptical reference to the events that brought him down: ". . . I have concluded that because of the Watergate matter I might not have the support of the Congress that I would consider necessary to back the very difficult decisions and carry out the duties of this office in the way the interests of the nation would require."

A listener who had not followed events might have supposed that a recalcitrant Congress, because of some not-too-important "matter," had somehow failed a President earnestly endeavoring to carry on for "peace and prosperity." The unaware listener would not have known that Nixon's only alternative to resignation was impeachment and removal from office—with the loss of a $60,000-a-year pension, $96,000 a year for staff and office expenses, free office space, free mailing privileges, and Secret Service aides.

All House Judiciary Committee members of both parties finally subscribed to one or more of the articles of impeachment. In each article was a paragraph containing the same words.

"SELF-DESTRUCTED"
June 5, 1974

"OOPS, OOP, AND AWAY"
June 13, 1974

THE PYRAMIDS AT HOME
June 14, 1974

At the time of Nixon's trip to Egypt.

"HOW WOULD EACH OF YOU FELLOWS LIKE A NUCLEAR REACTOR?"
June 18, 1974

On the news of Nixon's making available a nuclear reactor to Egypt and one to Israel.

June 19, 1974

ON THE TRAIL
June 21, 1974

This President elected as a law-and-order candidate had, in the words of the articles, acted "to the great prejudice of the cause of law and justice. . . ."

And in the same paragraphs of each of the articles of impeachment were words reminding me of the young congressman who had first come into my cartoons more than twenty-six years before, when he was pressing for passage of an "anti-subversive" bill:

"In all of this, Richard M. Nixon has acted contrary to his trust as President and subversive of constitutional government. . . ." ■

"CHIEF, THAT STONE WALL HAS HANDWRITING ON IT"
June 7, 1974

**"JUST A LITTLE FARTHER—
WE'RE ALMOST THERE"**

June 28, 1974

ANIMAL FARM, 1974

July 2, 1974

**"YOU SEE, HE'S NOT A COMMON
CRIMINAL LIKE US. HE WAS CHIEF
LAW-ENFORCEMENT OFFICER
OF THE U.S."**

June 9, 1974

In giving former Attorney General Richard Kleindienst a suspended sentence, U.S. District Judge George L. Hart, Jr., praised Kleindienst, whom he described as a man of "the highest integrity" and "universally respected and admired." He said of Kleindienst's failure to answer correctly under oath that "it reflects a heart that is loyal and considerate of others."

© 1974 HERBLOCK

BUBBLE DANCE

June 6, 1974

I've often summed up the essential role of the political cartoonist as being that of the kid in the Hans Christian Andersen story who says, "The emperor has no clothes on." For a long time after the Watergate break-in, it seemed to be a matter of saying, "Good grief, none of that bunch has any clothes on." There were a couple of occasions when it seemed appropriate to show the "emperor" literally in the buff.

"HELP! CALL THE PLUMBERS! SOMETHING'S BEEN LEAKED FROM A CONGRESSIONAL COMMITTEE!"

June 16, 1974

"IT'S A LITTLE IDEA WE GOT FROM THE KREMLIN"

July 5, 1974

"YOU WOULDN'T WALK OVER YOUR OWN LEADER, WOULD YOU?"

June 23, 1974

"THEN WE GET ANOTHER DELAY, THEN YOU GO ABROAD AGAIN, THEN THE FOREIGN LEADERS RETURN THOSE VISITS —THAT TAKES US UP TO THE BICENTENNIAL—"

July 3, 1974

"LEAN OVER BACKWARD JUST A LITTLE MORE SO YOU'LL APPEAR IN THE BEST LIGHT"

July 7, 1974

"PAT, HERE'S SOME GOOD REPUBLICAN CAMPAIGN FUND EARRINGS TO GO WITH THAT GOOD OLD RESPECTABLE REPUBLICAN CLOTH COAT"

July 12, 1974

"WE'VE MISMANAGED THE ECONOMY AGAIN, DEAR— WE DIDN'T INSIST ON PAYING MORE TAXES"

July 10, 1974

"BE FAIR! HOW ABOUT THE TIMES HE HAS NOT MADE PERSONAL USE OF CAMPAIGN FUNDS OR HIRED 'PLUMBERS' OR CHISELED ON HIS TAXES OR PROMOTED COVER-UPS . . ."

July 17, 1974

MISSING PART

July 11, 1974

THE OTHER COVER-UP

July 16, 1974

July 14, 1974

"IT KIND OF HELPS YOU UNDERSTAND HOW THEY MANAGED WATERGATE"

July 18, 1974

"YOU CLODS WILL TAKE WHAT WE GIVE YOU WHEN WE DECIDE TO GIVE IT TO YOU"

July 19, 1974

"HOW CAN THEY SAY HE HASN'T FAITHFULLY EXECUTED THE LAWS?"

July 21, 1974

"UH—YOU'RE NOT QUITE IN TUNE WITH US"

July 23, 1974

July 25, 1974

TIDAL WAVE
July 28, 1974

"JUMP"

July 24, 1974

**"SIR, HE SAYS HE HAS AN
APPOINTMENT WITH YOU"**

July 30, 1974

**"RELATIVELY SPEAKING, I'M
NOT DOING SO BAD"**

July 26, 1974

**"GEE, DOC, THEY TOLD ME YOU'D
CUT ME TO PIECES"**

July 31, 1974

INCH BY INCH

August 6, 1974

August 7, 1974

August 8, 1974

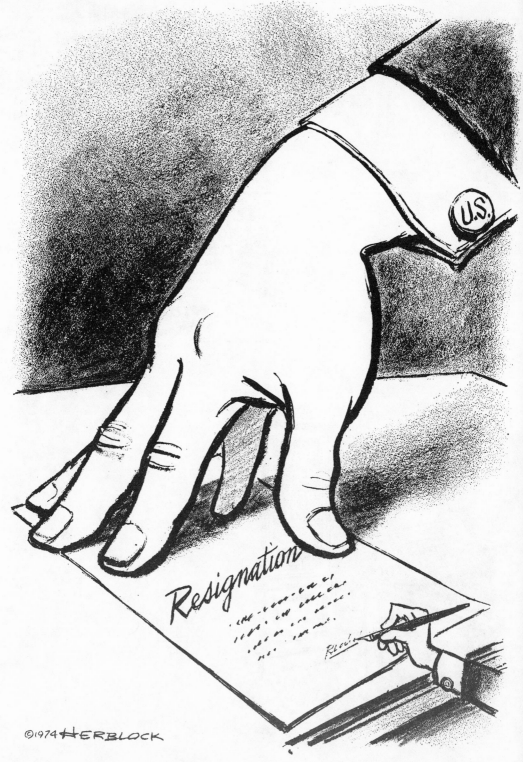

Resignation

©1974 HERBLOCK

August 9, 1974

AFTERWORD

When Nixon left office, there was a general sigh of relief. And in his first talk as President, Gerald Ford said that "our long national nightmare" was over. But one month later, in the Sunday morning statement that shocked the country, he said he could not "prolong the bad dreams that continue to reopen a chapter that is closed." So he issued a "full, free and absolute pardon unto Richard Nixon," and decided that Nixon should have control over access to White House tapes and documents. He thus insured that the nation's bad dreams would be prolonged far into the future.

Gerald Ford, in what columnist Mary McGrory called a Pearl Harbor "sneak attack on the due process and common sense," sought to still conscience forever with a sudden stunning blow, just as Richard Nixon tried to do in his "Saturday Night Massacre." Ford's attempt, like Nixon's, failed. But he did enormous damage to the nation.

Ford's secret decision proved, if proof were needed, how

shaky was the basis for the national self-congratulations of only a few weeks before on how well "the system worked."

A few flashbacks of events since Watergate show that the system worked in about the same way W. C. Fields captured a criminal in a movie: being unwittingly caught up in a chase, and finally winding up, by accident, sitting in a daze on the chest of the unconscious criminal.

The capture of the Watergate burglars involved a series of remarkable coincidences, as Fred Blumenthal wrote in *Parade* magazine. A watchman twice found a door taped open. The squad car which would normally respond in that area was temporarily out of commission, so the call was answered by an unmarked car manned by plainclothes detectives. And the burglars' lookout man stationed across the street paid no attention to them as they entered the building. By the time he saw the plainclothesmen with drawn guns searching through the building, he could not notify his confederates. By then, they had turned off their walkie-talkie to maintain silence.

Because it was a local break-in, *The Washington Post* assigned a couple of city reporters, under city editor Barry Sussman, to cover the story. And so Bob Woodward and Carl Bernstein pursued it as a crime story—all the way to the top.

A federal judge, John Sirica, happened to be in the right place at the right time. He also was not satisfied that the case involved only the defendants who appeared before him.

The disclosure that the White House tapes existed at all came about almost by accident—when assistant staff members to the Senate Watergate Committee were questioning a peripheral witness.

And the bit of tape that finally sealed Nixon's fate as President was hardly inevitable. With all the talk about mysterious disappearances and mysterious erasures of tapes, what was *more* mysterious was the existence of this evidence—unerased—incriminating even beyond anything previously disclosed.

There was even less reason to feel lucky about the responses of many Americans to these disclosures.

250

It's frightening that many Americans felt that *The President* should be supported whatever he did. It is even more frightening that in the face of all the evidence, Congress was reluctant to act until finally a prospective impeachment seemed safer than doing nothing. As noble as were the words and deeds of some House Judiciary Committee members, it seemed incredible that other members could for so long find nothing wrong at all. And a majority could not agree on more than three articles of impeachment to offer the Senate.

Until Nixon provided the last clinching impossible-to-overlook piece of evidence of his role in the cover-up six days after the Watergate break-in, many members of the U. S. Senate also had no desire to recognize what had gone on.

At the 1973 Senate Watergate hearings, Sen. Howard Baker (R-Tenn.) kept asking, "What did the President know and when did he know it?"

But as the answers began to be evident, he seemed to lose interest. Instead of pursuing questions about the President's involvement, Baker became more interested in establishing a CIA involvement with Watergate—which was what the White House, seeking a diversion, had tried to do from the beginning.

When the Senate Watergate Committee members wrote their reports in 1974, Baker issued a murky paper suggesting that more needed to be known about the CIA.

Sen. Hugh Scott (R-Pa.) had supported Nixon all the way. After Nixon left office, Scott was one of the first to call for forgetting the whole thing. Nixon, he said, had been "hung" and should not then be "drawn and quartered."

It was a strange kind of "hanging," in which President Ford shortly afterward asked Congress to appropriate $850,000 for Nixon. Of this, $450,000 was allotted for expenses related to an "orderly transition." The allotment for travel expenses was $40,000 and there was $100,000 for "miscellaneous."

It was a "hanging" that seemed more like payday at the mill.

Meanwhile Spiro Agnew was already complaining of being treated harshly for what he called "my decision not to contest" one tax charge—words that should have served as a warning of things to come.

Those who had done nothing to stop the spreading national infection now sought to bind up the nation's wounds —with the infection still there. They wanted to avoid national division—by creating a situation in which the nation might be forever torn on whether this President had really committed serious offenses, or whether any President should be subject to penalties. Here was a formula not for ending a nightmare but for continuing one.

There were some—like Sen. Lowell Weicker (R-Conn.) and Albert Jenner, Jr., counsel to the Republican minority on the House impeachment inquiry—who had been capable of voicing conscience and of putting the nation before party, politics, or President. But there should have been many more.

Rep. James Mann (D-S.C.) of the House Judiciary Committee made a thoughtful observation: "Next time there may be no watchman in the night."

What if next time there should be no watchman, no persistent reporters, no suspicious judge—and no tapes?

The answer is not encouraging, especially after all the expressions of sympathy which followed first Agnew and then Nixon when they left their respective offices.

It is hardly vindictive to ask why men who betrayed positions of the highest trust should not even be required to enter a guilty plea. It would hardly be a good precedent if those who achieved the highest offices were deemed immune to anything but the possible loss of those high jobs.

Elliot Richardson, William Ruckelshaus, and other men of honor lost positions in government—for *being* men of honor.

Those who were so greatly concerned about the resigned President and Vice President acted as if the high positions and emoluments *belonged* to the Nixons and Agnews—as if they were heroes whose laurels had somehow unfortunately, even unfairly, been snatched from them.

Compassion is due all criminals. There are the luckless poor and ignorant who spend much of their lives in jail for minor crimes. But Nixon and Agnew showed a remarkable lack of compassion for such people—while committing their own crimes because of a greed for money and power which could not be satisfied even with the large salaries, special privileges, and honors of the highest offices in the nation.

Yet there was much talk about the "tragedy" that those who had risen so high should have fallen—as if we were marking the passing of kings.

The tragedy is not that those who rose so high should fall so low. The tragedy is that those who had so low an appreciation for our government should have risen to such high positions in it.

That they were elected for "four more years" may have been partly due to the fact that Nixon was able to delay congressional hearings on the scandals until after the 1972 election. In the second Nixon administration, the nation endured more than a year of trauma—during which it was constantly told that a remedy would be traumatic.

And so, belatedly and after a fashion, things seemed to be working out. Even then, it might be said of Watergate, as the Duke of Wellington said of Waterloo, that it was a damn close thing.

But it was not over.

As Americans were relaxing and enjoying their good fortune on coming through the crisis, there was the smashing blow of the new President's 8th-of-September statement.

The Gerald Ford—who, at the hearings on his confirmation to be Vice President, had said that "the public wouldn't stand for" a possible Nixon pardon, and who only days earlier had said clemency would be reserved while the law went forward—this Gerald Ford now suddenly issued an irrevocable pardon to his predecessor for all offenses—known and unknown.

It was as if he regarded offenses against the public as none of the public's business. In judging that Nixon had "suffered enough," he punished still further an already suffering nation.

The New York Times said:

> President Ford speaks of compassion. It is tragic that he had no compassion and concern for the Constitution and the Government of law that he has sworn to uphold

253

© 1974 HERBLOCK

THE LONG NATIONAL NIGHTMARE GOES ON
September 12, 1974

and defend. He could probably have taken no single act of a non-criminal nature that would have more gravely damaged the credibility of this Government in the eyes of the world and of its own people than this unconscionable act of pardon.

The speech was boggling to Americans who thought credibility had at last been restored to the Oval Office.

Ford said: "I deeply believe in equal justice for all Americans whatever their station or former station"—and went on to show that he believed in no such thing.

He talked about the danger of passions being aroused and of opinions polarized—and proceeded to arouse passions and to polarize the people. He spoke of ensuring domestic tranquility —and created domestic turmoil.

And he said that he, as President, was exercising his power "to firmly shut and seal this book."

And so the idea of some kind of divine right of Presidents went on.

The cover-up went on.

What about the future of Watergate, and Watergates of the future?

Ours, we are always told, is a government of laws, not of men. But the laws don't enforce themselves. The public itself has to be a watchman in the night, keeping such a sharp lookout that public servants find it easier to do the right thing than the wrong thing.

The late Doris Fleeson, one of the best columnists ever, summed it up in a speech. She told her audience:

"I wish I had some magic formula to suggest. There is none. There are no wonder men or wonder women. There are only you and I and others who believe in freedom." ■

© 1974 HERBLOCK

"... I, AS PRESIDENT, HAVE THE CONSTITUTIONAL POWER TO FIRMLY SHUT AND SEAL THIS BOOK."
—GERALD R. FORD,
PARDON SPEECH, SEPTEMBER 8, 1974